Winning th

Winning the Race

Samuel Kasumu

RoperPenberthy Publishing

Published by RoperPenberthy Publishing Ltd, Springfield House,
23 Oatlands Drive, Weybridge, Surrey KT13 9LZ

Text copyright © Samuel Kasumu, 2012

ISBN 978 1 903905 76 0

Cover artwork by Michael Masade Jr. of Maestro Creative
Cover portrait photography by Ayo Oduniyi of AO Media

Typeset by Avocet Typeset, Chilton, Aylesbury, Bucks.

Printed in England

CONTENTS

Introduction

Following years of procrastination, I am so pleased to be introducing to you a book that I hope will inspire the next generation. I guess my story so far is one that is a mixture of both the ordinary and the extraordinary. Born into a pretty normal African home, with parents who were quite traditional, I am the fourth of five siblings with the same mother and father, and have a number of half-brothers and sisters. My parents separated when I was around 8 years old, so I was brought up in a single parent household that struggled financially throughout my childhood. For a large part of the UK population this is a very common story. Eventually I ended up at university, and I guess this is where the extraordinary kicks in.

My university experience was a turning point in my life. I managed to break my hands on Bomb Fire Night, become President of the largest African & Caribbean Society in the UK, break student union election records, start an organisation, and enter the world of politics... all within the space of 4 years. At some point within those years I managed to join the Conservative Party.

Looking back, I think that I have been very fortunate to have experienced the many things that I have in my life to date. They have helped to shape who I am, and they are the reason for what I will become tomorrow. I am a young black Conservative who is a Christian and is respected by a diversity of influencers across the country. Five descriptive words (young, black, Conservative, Christian, respected) seldom form a collective description of any individual. It is therefore my hope that the book that you are about to read gives you a better understanding of why I have arrived at My Personal Creed!

The title of this book 'Winning the Race' has many levels

to it. My dream of one day reaching the pinnacle of UK politics is just one of the many things that I hope to achieve. I once said to a Member of Parliament that winning is relative. The MP first disagreed with me, but when I explained how I arrived at this conclusion he soon changed his mind. Ultimately winning means different things to different people, but for me the overriding theme of winning is about the difference you can make. It's about how much of your gifts and talents you are able to use to serve others for the greater good.

I guess another thing to say before you read this book is that normal is also relative. I believe that many of us in this world have a story to tell, but for so many we forget that our norm is both unique in context and expression. The themes and experiences of this book will probably relate to so many people in different ways. I'll be telling as best I can my story, not with the intention to boast or to glorify some of the things that I have been unfortunate to do, but to set the scene for the future. I'll also want to show how eternal principles have led to some forms of success for me, and can do for many others. The truth is that living is not the challenge... living a life of purpose and drawing strength from a conviction is. The hope is that this book will allow for the above statement to be true.

I would like to first and foremost thank Jehovah, my Lord and saviour, for my faith has been the lamp unto my feet. I must also say that this book may never have been written if it wasn't for the lady that has stolen my heart so unexpectedly. Barbara, my wife, was the motivation behind getting me to start making this happen, and for this I shall be eternally grateful.

Section 1:

Humble Beginnings

Chapter 1

Early Years

I was born the fourth of a family of five. I was the most quiet of my siblings, and was made very aware of this distinction growing up. I had behavioural and learning difficulties at school, and was one of the students that would leave my peers in primary school for 'special needs' classes. I must say however that I am very fortunate for even being in a primary school class as I was expelled from nursery at the age of 3. I am said to have physically assaulted the nursery teacher at the time, as well been highly disruptive in the class. Over the years I found it particularly challenging to accept that I was bad enough to have been expelled from a nursery, but having looked back to the earliest memories of my childhood I think that I could understand why I may have been so aggressive. For the very first thing I can remember is witnessing domestic violence. Witnessing such scenes could of course help to show me just where I had learnt to be quite aggressive in my early years. As the first boy in the house I guess it was expected that I would be a bit of a naughty child, but at times my behaviour extreme.

Eventually I was admitted into a new school, and began year one at Dock on a Hill Primary. I can't remember doing much work, but what I can remember is that I wasn't there too long. Having missed out on pre-school education, I was already quite behind in regards to my development. I was also born in late August, and as a result was one of the youngest in my class too. Soon it was once again time to leave, but this time it wasn't for my behaviour. My parents had decided to relocate to Nigeria, and we all packed our bags and were off to Lagos. We arrived in the evening, and my sister Victoria began to throw up soon after our arrival. The air was very humid and the whole atmosphere from the airport was very tense. Vicki was always the one that would get ill very easily, but this time my other two sisters followed suit. We were in a car close to armed men in what looked like military uniform. It was all a very scary welcome to this new environment and I was very glad when we eventually reached our new home where dad had arrange for a 'Welcome' sign to be plastered on a fish tank. Life was a bit different here, as we seemed to be wealthier in this new country. Our house had gates and quite a few rooms, which was certainly larger in comparison to the small South London flat that was our previous family home. Nigeria is a place where the gap between the haves and have not's is very visible. I remember seeing so many people on the streets begging on the sidewalks. I had never seen anything like it in England. With a population of around 150 million people it is a place that in many respects is so much bigger than the UK. Perhaps the time when I went was very different to the Nigeria that we have today. Its democracy has made a lot of progress, with its first free and fair elections in 2011. Nigeria is now a great emerging market, and in another 20 years, at its current rate of growth, we can be sure that it will not be too far behind being a super power. But of course it still has to deal with many of the challenges linked to poverty.

We stayed in Nigeria for around 6 or 7 months altogether, but it felt like a lifetime. Everything was different; that is everything except my school experience. I was given a blue uniform and sent to a school called 'Tender Touch'. In a country where smacking in school is still permitted (and in many cases encouraged) being sent to a school called 'Tender Touch' left little to the imagination. I was dropped off by my parents and within a few minutes the same behaviour that had led to my nursery exclusion manifested again. The school initially put me into a class that I refused to remain in, and my violent protest resulted in me being put into one of the other form groups. A young lady in the class decided it wise to mock the way that I spoke and the other children found it all quite amusing. I concluded that she was not going to have the last laugh... picked up my bag... and used all of my strength to swing for her head. I cannot remember whether or not the bag made a connection, but it certainly spelt the end of my time within that class room. I was moved forcefully back to the original class, and this was where I remained until we came back to England. To say that I was one of the dumbest members of the class is very much an understatement. I would get exceptionally bad grades and would not understand most of the things being taught. The young people were far more advanced than me, and were learning concepts that I could barely grasp. There's not much else besides school that I remember about Nigeria. The domestic violence never stopped, there were loads of insects and lizards which looked like little dinosaurs, and we would eat meat that was so fresh that you would literally see the goat, chicken, or turkey, alive the day that you ate it. That was pretty much all I can remember of our 6 or 7 months in Nigeria.

One day, my father travelled on one of his business trips I think, and mum decided that this was her time to act. She had been saving up some money, and used it to purchase tickets to fly all of us back to London. She had had enough of Nigeria! Looking back, it must have cost her quite a bit of money to fly 5 children over, and I am very grateful that she did this, but till this day I think it is something that hurts my father very much. It probably helped to spell the end of our family unit. We arrived back in London in the summer of 1996. We stayed with a relative in East Finchley. I don't think I had ever been to North London before this, and so it was quite different to what I was used to in the UK before we had left. Our relative was so kind to allow six new tenants into what was not a very large flat. She already had a few people living with her which made it all quite a tight affair. Eventually we got our own place in North Finchley, and I attended Northside Primary on Percy Road. I got into my fair share of fights at school as you do, and would disrupt the class regularly. I hung around with some older kids in the local playground after school and on the weekends, which was quite cool for me at the time. Sometimes they'd encourage me to start fights with some of the other young boys in the area, and I would duly oblige. Dad eventually came to London and moved in with us for about a year or so, and then my parents officially separated. It wasn't really much of an emotional separation as both my parents had been frequent travellers, and I had never seen my father for a sustainable period of time anyway. Nigeria was probably the only time we had what was close to a strong family unit that I could remember, but this of course lasted only a few months. I remember my younger brother seeing my dad one time when we were really young, and him saying "hello uncle". He had never known my father long enough to recognise him as his dad, and he needed to be told who he was. After my parent's separation, we would move house very frequently as my Mother struggled to support herself and five children financially. She was a businesswoman, who had made money in the past through buying and selling gold and other fashion items but it was becoming increasingly difficult to balance her business with being a single parent. Business was all she really knew how to do, and having previously been quite successful she found it very difficult to think of alternatives. As a result, there came times when we would have no adult supervision at all for months as my mum worked hard to make the business work, and the eldest sister in the house would have to assume the role of parent.

Secondary school was much of the same really. I had chosen to attend a school called Christ Church because two of my friends said that they would also be going, only for one to migrate back to Cyprus, and the other to move outside London. By the time I was made aware that they would no longer be attending this school it was too late for me to change my mind. I was off to one of the worst schools in the borough and nobody from my Primary School would be following me there. True to form, I was a bit of a handful for the teachers. I believe I was suspended from school every year that I was there, and accrued a large number of detentions. The school was fun and I did feel very at home but of course it was not the best environment for academic attainment. Christ Church was performing below average in school league tables, and had gone into special measures as a result. Mum would give me one pound a day and I had a choice of whether I would spend it on getting the 40 pence bus to and from school, or whether I would use it to buy some sweets and walk to school instead. I was on free school meals, which at the time never really felt like a bad thing as so were many of the other kids. Christ Church was based in Finchley, however many of the students would come from neighbouring Brent and Haringey. A lot of the parents would send their children to the school in the hope that they would get a better education in an area that had better schools. Race wasn't really an issue in the school because it was so diverse, however there were times when we'd do some really silly things like have football matches that were 'blacks against whites'. The few times that this happened fights would eventually break out, but by the next day all would return to normal.

I lasted two and a half years in Christ Church and in year 9 I had a day that I would never forget. I was playing football in the playground when one of the teaching assistants started a fight with me. I can't remember the reason but I'm sure he probably felt he had a justification (God knows why a teaching assistant would ever feel justified in doing something so stupid). I went to a room to write a statement about what had happened, then I caught glimpse of a young man that I regularly chased to give a few punches. I got up and chased him around the school, disrupting lessons, and was caught by the head teacher who suspended me for three days on the spot. When it was time to return to the school they requested a meeting with my Mother before I could return to lessons. My Mother was of course outside of the country on one of her business trips, and even if she was in the country there would be no way that I could explain to her that I had been suspended for the third time. My Mother hadn't even been to a parents evening since I was in year 7 as it was far too risky for me to let her hear what I had been up to. This was long before Labour had implemented new laws on smacking, and even if those laws existed they certainly would have had no value in my house.

So I did the unthinkable, I became a habitual truant and missed well over a month of school through staying on buses and visiting video game shops. I met a fellow truant (who would later end up in prison as a repeat offender) and developed a rhythm to my day. The school allowed me to take my SATs tests, but this was the last thing I did at Christ Church C of E School. I had witnessed many other pupils having to leave through being expelled, and the fear that I would one day have to leave due to something linked to my behaviour had finally come to realisation. Within a few years Christ Church was shut as it was unable to improve following a long period on special measures. I was merely one of many students that had let the school down. Maybe Christ Church School had actually let me down too. When I was in Primary School I had been getting extra support for what was identified as learning difficulties, but at Christ Church I was just another student that was disruptive. Maybe if they had been able to identify the challenges I was having earlier the outcomes would have been different, who knows. I would not want to blame anyone for my behaviour and probably was fortunate to have lasted in the school as long as I did. If it was another school it is likely that they would have moved me on much sooner.

Eventually my Mother's cousin helped me to apply for a new school as we had moved home again. Lee Valley was the name of the new place I attended, which was based in Enfield. The school had a large ethnic minority population like Christ Church, but this time it consisted mainly of Turkish and African & Caribbean students. Academically, it was actually worse than Christ Church. 17.5% of the students in the school left with 5 good GCSE's and there were several instances where weapons were involved in violent attacks. My first day was certainly interesting, as I witnessed one student being cut with a blade, and the victim responding by taking a large knife from his bag to chase the person that had cut him. Christ Church was a very bad school, but even the bad kids weren't bad enough to do such things on the playground at lunchtime. This was a completely new level of youth violence from what I was used to, so I had to adapt and I had to adapt fast. Being true to form, on my first day of school I managed to get a letter home about concerns that a teacher had with my behaviour. By this time mum had come back from her travels and she was far from impressed. I received her full force and was given a range of punishments that would leave me sweating like I had just ran a marathon... in a desert.

So I was in a tough school; by this time living in Edmonton' quite a tough area, in a single parent home, I was well on the way to becoming another statistic. Things could have turned out very different for me if it wasn't for God... literally! Two of my sister's and little brother had started to attend a church in Finchley Road at the time. They'd come home with stories of what had happened in church, and it all sounded pretty fascinating. So one day I decided to follow them in order to see what all the fuss was about. I walked into this church which was full of African & Caribbean people that were quite friendly. By this time we lived in an area where my experiences of people were quite different. Where I lived it was common practice for young men like me to have an aggressive and standoffish aura. It was almost like survival mode, as the hope was people would avoid attempting to rob you if you looked intimidating yourself. The church service began and people passionately sang and danced with great emotion. After the Pastor had finished preaching his sermon, he asked what I thought was a very deep question. He said 'if you were to die today, where would you go?' He began to speak about how many people thought they would go to heaven, but according to the Christian faith you needed to be Born Again. He went on to explain that heaven would only accept those that believed in their heart and accepted with their mouth that Jesus Christ was the son of God, and that such a proclamation would lead to a change in the course of one's destiny. I left the church with great food for thought, but did not take the required steps that he had instructed.

The next week I went back to the church, and this time the preacher had travelled and a Bishop from America had come to take the service. This gentleman's name was Bishop Kenneth Ulmer. He had a mega church in Los Angeles, and would preach a message equally as convincing as the week before. At the end of the sermon he asked a similar question, and this time I decided to take that step forward. I went forward, I said the prayer, I became a Born Again Christian, and I was without a doubt on cloud nine. They gave me a New Testament Bible which also had the Old Testament book of Proverbs, and a tape which I made sure to listen to. So just before my 13th birthday I had committed to living a life as a Christian and I was determined to make sure that I lived right as best I could. I began to erase swearing from my normal expression, although there were certainly many hiccups along the way. I also decided that I would be a bit better behaved when it came to engaging with females, an area that I must admit had far more hiccups along the way in comparison to my swearing problem. I fell in love with the book of Proverbs in the Bible, and I developed a passion for wisdom. I began to change and mature as a person, however there was, and I guess still is, much more room for improvement.

We soon moved house again and I moved schools one last time. At this point I had been to three schools within two and a half terms. I knew that I had to move away from Lee Valley in order to improve my chances of doing well. We moved to Barnet, and when I told my friends where we were moving to they would keep on saying, "there's National Front racists in that area." It did get me a bit apprehensive but we had no choice but to move as the council had given us a new property. I ended up at a school called East Barnet. I remember walking in for the first time and seeing a sign saying '*I Want to Learn*'. I then looked into a class room window and saw to my surprise students actually doing work. There was so much order and even silence in the corridors. It was the strangest experience and I genuinely thought I would not last long in this new school. I remember thinking the school reminded me of Grange Hill. I did not trust that my behaviour would improve sufficiently to avoid expulsion. Even though I was now a Christian, I was still very much in the process of character reform. The culture was very different in this school, and so was the ethnic makeup. The majority of the school were white, which meant that I automatically stood out. Strangely, a young man who was also black began school on the same day as me and was also in the same class as me. I'm not sure how this happened, but if it wasn't for this young man I may have had a very terrible time in the school indeed. Of course if it wasn't for him, maybe I would have integrated into the school a lot faster. I had someone that was from the same background, that I could relate to, and as a result the new environment was a bit easier to handle. The kids in the school took to our arrival in different ways. For some of the females we were potentially the fulfilment of some strange fantasy and we had superstar status. For some of the Greek constituents within the school we were potential allies within what I could only describe as a break down in race relations. And for a lot of the white British young men in the school, we became an automatic threat for both of the above reasons.

Some of the white boys in the school certainly did not make us feel very welcome initially, and there were regular build ups to potential fights after school. Thankfully these fights never manifested, but this was the first time that I had ever experienced direct racial tensions of this sort. In my previous schools I was part of a majority, I attended a black majority church, and most of my immediate associates were black. Till this day I'm not sure if I could qualify what I experienced as racism, mainly because of what the term represents to me. It represents one group being able to exert a form of power over another. In my school we gave as good as we got, and yes race did play a part in this, but I was never adversely affected. It's quite strange that today I see some of the same young boys that made it quite clear that we were not welcome at the school and we say hello to each other. I'm not too sure what their thoughts are of me now, but I do feel like it has highlighted how big the role of ignorance plays in any form of racial tensions.

Thankfully I never got excluded, and I stayed on at East Barnet School for the Sixth Form. This was much more peaceful and I developed friendships with many of the people in what was a very small Sixth Form. I decided to study A Levels in Business, History, and Drama. The thinking behind my choices was that I wanted to own a business one day, I was an aspiring actor, and I was really good at history. My behaviour had improved slightly by this stage, but I was still very much an unconventional student. I didn't live too far from the school but punctuality was a big issue. One of my teachers was a lady called Miss Smith who was from South Africa. Although I was very disruptive in her lessons, it was very evident that she showed me a lot of favour. I think this was because of a combination of me being black and me getting very good marks for my work. I would arrive in the class late, be very disruptive, and answer questions with ease all at the same time. Miss Smith would in turn joke with me, give me good marks, and send me out of the class all in equal measure. She would be a teacher that I retained a relationship with for years after I left the school and I would be firmly fixed as her favourite ever student.

Sixth Form is where school got rather interesting when it came to females too. Suddenly I was surrounded by girls from a very different culture to what I was used to at church and at home. These girls would go out and get drunk quite a bit and were quite sexually active. I was now part of their community to an extent, but at the same time I wasn't. I still hung out with the guy that I had started school with on the same day, and we were not willing fully to buy into this culture of sex, drugs, and alcohol. There was a particular girl in the year above that was very keen to take my virginity. She was known for being very sexually active, and in fact was said to have had sexual relations with some very prominent Premier League football players. When she realised that I was still a virgin she made it her mission to attempt to have her wicked way with me. It wasn't easy, but I managed to last the whole of the Sixth Form without doing 'IT'. Playing a lot football and Playstation meant that I had hobbies that could hold my attention. There were however, some very interesting moments when things did get rather heated with some of my fellow female sixth formers. Throughout my time in East Barnet School & Sixth Form I had only had one girlfriend, a Greek girl in the year below who I had previously met in my drama classes at Boden's Theatre School. I had been an aspiring actor at this point, and began doing small roles on programmes like East Enders before moving onto a better agency where I started to audition for more important roles. I didn't like being treated as a second class citizen, which was how you would sometimes be treated if you weren't the main actor on sets. The relationship with this lovely Greek lady lasted a whole two and half weeks. I also had my first real kiss whilst at Sixth Form. This was with a lady that had also attended East Barnet School, but actually left a few months after I had arrived. We would later have a relationship at university where she would break my heart.

So my early years were normal in many respects, but also helped me to understand different communities. I had been to three distinct schools with very different characteristics. I had lived in two different countries and in South, East, and North London. I had experienced a variety of cultures and interacted with very different types of people. If we are products of our environments, then I would reckon such variety is what has led to my own ability to engage with different people from different backgrounds. Although one would question the validity of that statement when you hear what I did next...

In the final year of my Sixth Form I decided that I was to attend Imperial College. I had achieved 2 A's and 1B at AS Level and I believed that I had the grades to fulfil this ambition. I applied to study Business at Imperial and was duly given an offer. I went to visit their campus and remember feeling very uncomfortable. The first thing I realised was that there weren't many people that looked like me on the campus, and those that did seemed to be from abroad (international students). The second thing that I realised was that the course that I chose would be very intense and demanding. I was still an aspiring actor at this stage and thought that there was no way that I could commit to such tough working conditions and also live amongst people that seemed very different to me. When it came to the time for me to pick my university, I rejected Imperial College, and chose the only other credible option on my UCAS form; Brunel University. It was a university that I had never visited, nor knew much about. I only knew that most people had warned me not to go there because apparently the students were just party animals and I was told the campus had an 'urban' feel to it. People warned me that I wouldn't like it, and that it was not the type of place that suited my character. Looking back, it was clear that I had used the same method of selection that many other students with the same background as me have done in the past.

In 2011, 43% of students that lived in London who were black stayed in London for university. This was in contrast to only 3% of white students. Many young people were, and still are, increasingly choosing to stay in their comfort zones and as a result were not going to the best universities available. For some reason, black students were making choices that would make them anti-competitive within the labour market, but no one was there to give the advice needed for them to make more informed decisions. By the time I decided to change my choice it was too late. I tried everything that I could, and was even considering using the UCAS' Clearing system to get into a better university. Studying History at Kings College University was amongst the alternative courses that I considered. Eventually I decided to stick with the choice that I had made, and in September 2005 I began my journey at Brunel University, studying a degree in Business & Management Accounting. This was where I would literally enter a new chapter in my life. Something told me that although people thought I had made a bad decision, Brunel

University was where I was meant to be. It was the right next step for my personal journey.

Chapter 2

Entering the Unknown

I arrived on Brunel University campus on a sunny September Sunday afternoon. It was a long drive to Uxbridge, a part of West London that I had never been to before. My Mother dropped me off with my sister Victoria and little brother Philip. Victoria had a friend who was a final year student at Brunel and she was also kind enough to help with my move onto campus. This was the first time that I had ever seen Brunel and it seemed like such a big campus. When we were walking through I was in my natural reflective mood, taking everything in. Philip however seemed to be way more excited about the experience than me, and people kept asking if he was the family member moving in. This of course made my 15 year old little brother very happy indeed, and his very large smile confirmed his joy at being considered a fellow university first year 'fresher'. I'm sure it added greatly to his desire to one day go to university too. There were so many large buildings and so many people. Some of the students from older years were on campus to help us new students, but I had the feeling that they also had their own motives for meeting some of the new females on campus. We went to collect the keys to my new room and then went to move my things in. I was to stay in Clifton Halls off Residence- Block N. As soon as we got to my block a friendly looking guy came to introduce himself. I could tell straight away that he was a Nigerian, which was strange because I'm normally not that good at telling these things. I guess him greeting my mother with the traditional Nigeria courtesy bow gave it away a bit. He introduced himself to my family and my mother was a bit more at ease knowing that someone from her native country would be in the same block as me.

After putting all my stuff away in my new home, the family sat down for a few minutes, and then Victoria instructed everyone to start leaving. She was adamant that it was now time for me to have some fun, and everyone was cramping my style. My Mother was evidently not ready to leave me (mentally or physically) but eventually she was convinced to start to make her way back to the car. I walked the family to the car park and listened to the last few instructions of what not to do by my Mother. We said our very emotional good-byes and then I was left on my own. It was a pretty emotional walk back to my room from the car park, and I remember having a feeling of not knowing what would happen next. The anxiety that one feels when one chapter comes to an end and another chapter begins was very much the feeling that I had. I was now by myself with no safety net of a large family or a group of friends that I had been around for a good few years. My church was no longer around the corner, and it was time for me to meet some new people. Thankfully there was a young man that I knew from my area. He was known for being part of one of the most feared gangs in my borough, of which one of my closest friends was also a member. He came to visit me in my halls and I was thankful that I had someone from my area to associate with. We went to the first Fresher's Party in the campus nightclub which was rather interesting. We also met some of the people within my block and began to make some new friends. Unfortunately the boy from my area did not fully embrace this new challenge and before the week had ended he would move back to Barnet. I'm not sure why he chose to move out so quickly, but I suspect that he did not really like being in a place where his reputation was not as strong, and where he never had the safety net of being around his fellow gang members.

I did have another friend from my area, a young man from East Barnet School. He was called Sam Barnes, and was in my History and Drama A-Level classes in my Sixth Form. We needed a way to differentiate him from me, so eventually he was given the nickname by my friends of 'white boy Sam' or just 'white Sam'. He embraced the name too, however I'm not too sure what the reaction would have been if I had been called 'black boy Sam' by his friends. Within two days of Fresher's Week everybody seemed to have located their own groups to form new communities. People from different ethnic backgrounds would locate each other, as well as people with different cultures. Sam Barnes and I would have a relationship that helped to bridge racial barriers. For some of my peers I am sure he was the only white male that they would engage with regularly, and they really took a liking to him. They thought he was very crazy, and was very fascinated by him and his friends' use of drugs. Sam was very free spirited and embraced different people, and I believe he really appreciated me for my Christian faith and respected me for having principles that I stuck too.

Fresher's Week was a very new environment to what I was used to. As a Christian virgin that did not regularly go to night clubs, I was in an environment where everyone seemed to go out and be very liberated when it came to sexual relations. The young Nigerian guy that I met when I first arrived on campus, John, was no different. He quickly became my closest friend on campus, and people used his name as way of identifying which Sam they were speaking about (an alternative to being called black Sam of course). So I was called John's Sam. John had the first ever Fresher's house party in his room, and was very free with the ladies. He was from Kennington in South London, and had gotten a scholarship to study at a private boarding school. This meant that he was very comfortable with different types of people, and was quite liberal to say the least. I found myself tempted by this new found liberalism that I was seeing and eventually wanted my own share of the fun. There was a young lady two floors up from our floor that was quite attractive. One evening I decided that I would invite myself to her room and told her in advance that I'd be coming. I went upstairs, and to my surprise she had brought out what looked like a condom and placed it on the table. I guess she thought that a guy inviting himself into a room at night could only suggest one course of action considering the context of the week we were in, but I was quite naive. I'm not sure what I thought would happen once I got up there. It was all a bit new to me. Eventually the lights were taken off and we went into bed. We started to talk, and eventually I explained that I was a virgin. I think she was very surprised, said it was cute and we went to sleep. Just before we went to sleep however, we spoke about Christianity, and she explained that she was trying to live a Christian life and did not wish to engage in promiscuous behaviour whilst at university. Looking at the condom in her room, I had a feeling that she felt like this would be a challenge too strong with all the temptations on a campus, and as a result she had prepared just in case. It seemed as she had felt that night would be the first night that signified the defeat of her will power, and she would both experience some pleasure and pain. She had survived another night of campus celibacy, and I had probably missed a chance to take something someone was preparing to give. I was very perplexed as to how I felt about the situation, and eventually went back to my room downstairs.

As Fresher's Week carried on John and I decided to go to an event being held by the African & Caribbean Society (ACS) on campus. This was a society for students that were either of African or Caribbean decent, or shared an interest in this community. I had previously gone to a barbecue that they had put on a few days earlier, and everyone else was going so we tagged along. The event was in one of the lecture rooms and was called 'Homecoming'. The title reminded me of American style fraternities and I thought that this would be what I experienced. Unfortunately this wasn't the case. I can't remember too much about what happened at the event, but I can remember there being some form of talent show where people from the audience could come to the front to demonstrate their talent. A guy came to the front and began to dance to some reggae music. The crowd didn't seem to be very impressed by his display of talent and there was an uncomfortable silence. He could see that he wasn't getting any love, and decided to ask for any lady in the crowd to join him in order for him to show his gyrating skills. What happened next would shock almost everyone in the room. He began to swing the girl on the table, and attempted to turn her upside down. Some of the hosts ran to break up this strange looking incident, and this was probably the moment when I said to myself that I wanted nothing to do with this society. I did not sign up as a member, and did not attend their subsequent events. I returned to my room very disgusted by the fact that a society that was designed to demonstrate positive aspects of African & Caribbean culture had little style or substance. Of course I was just a first year student at this time and had very limited power to do anything about this so proceeded to carry on with my Fresher's Week.

Towards the end of the week the initial rush had begun to go and I started to return to my normal mannerisms. I never returned to the campus nightclub again that week; however the challenge with females did not subside. Quite a lot of people had come to Brunel from South London and a lot of them knew my new friend John. The people from South London seemed to have a distinctive look. You could tell that they were from there as they kind of spoke differently. I find it quite interesting how people from York can tell when someone is from Leeds because of how they speak, and this was a similar experience for me as someone from North London. I was of course from Barnet, and it became a bit more evident to me that I did not completely share the same social experiences as my new friends.

There was one girl that I found particularly fascinating. She was very tomboyish. For some strange reason I took a liking to her loud nature and very soon we got close. She came over to see John in our block one evening and I took her to my room where she remained for most of the evening. We kissed quite a bit and then almost like déjà vu she began to tell me how she was a Christian that wanted to live for Christ and desperately did not want to get involved with any guys in a sexual nature during her time at university. Looking back, I think maybe I should have taken these moments as some sort of sign. Maybe something, or someone, was telling me to avoid getting into such situations. The next evening I went to her room and we carried on from where we left off. This time we were going further than I had ever done with a female before and I told her I was a virgin. That evening she took my virginity. She seemed quite upset at the whole situation after we were done to be honest, and I left her to go back to my room where I duly boasted to John about how I had just had sex with his friend. Of course he never knew that I was a virgin at the time, and just took it as me also embracing the liberal nature of a university campus. I had come to university without any preconceived ideas as to what to expect. I'm very sure that I did not expect to lose my virginity within the first few weeks, and I am very sure that I didn't imagine being in such a crisis of faith. This was all a very different experience and I should have made more of an effort to find people with similar values to my own. I'm sure this would have at least helped me to avoid compromising the things I cared so much about.

Looking back, I believe that I put myself in a very vulnerable position and this is exactly what most young people do when they leave home to go to university. No one really gave me the advice I needed in regards to how to stay true to my personal beliefs. There were just too many negative influences around me, and I would have been much better prepared if I had a mentor or been in constant communication with people that were more mature than me. I also think that there was an inevitable risk of me staying on campus. Perhaps I should have stayed at home and commuted. The benefits would be that I would have been less tempted to compromise, but I guess at the same time if I never stayed on campus, the rest of this book may not have been written. For campus was the launch pad for most of what I learnt and achieved in the subsequent years. My first few weeks were probably similar to what most young people go through once they enter the new environment of a university campus. It's a defining moment in a person's life when they cross over from kid-hood to adulthood. Although most of us believe that we can handle such changes, the truth is that we need people around us to help us through. We are all human and susceptible to mistakes, but with a strong support network we're much more likely to be successful in every area of our lives. Another friend of mine from my area actually came to Brunel too, and we had very similar values. For some strange reason we ended up not really seeing each other whilst at university. Being around him more would have certainly helped the situation. He was part of the Christian Union, and I would see them handing out tea to students in the evenings and evangelising on campus. I chose another path to him and had to deal with the outcomes. It was now time for me to go home for the weekend and then to continue my academic year proper when I returned.

Strangely I quickly built a reputation for being a bit of a bad boy on campus; however I still had my reserved nature and stayed in my room in Clifton Block N most of the time. I began to have regular acquaintances with females but never went all the way again. Some girls would cook for me (as cooking was a key area of weakness that I had) and other girls would clean up my room. One female student in particular was very good at colour coordinating the clothes in my wardrobe. I knew that a few of the girls had developed strong feelings for me, and used this to my advantage. They liked the fact that I was very serious about my faith and had a very deep passion for wisdom which I had developed years ago. I used to pin up famous quotes on my wall, and also had the whole of Martin Luther King's 'I Have a Dream' speech on my shelf. MLK was, and still is, my inspiration. I was still relatively inexperienced when it came to ladies; some of the other boys in my block were far more used to being very promiscuous with females. My next door neighbour was a guy called Ian from Leicester who shared the same birthday as me. He was mixed race, and a lot of the girls took a liking to him early on. To many of the African Caribbean girls' disgust, he wasn't too keen on them and instead preferred a blonde or a brunet. He would quickly become friends with my friend Sam (white Sam), and they partied most evenings. Ian would regularly bring home different ladies that he had met at the night club and boast of the night's activities the next day or sometimes just after the young lady had left. We never slept in Clifton till around 3am most nights, and 9am lectures were never really a realistic option for Ian and I. One of us would knock on the other's door to ask if we were going. We'd then confirm to each other that we were both not interested in attending and would carry on sleeping till late into the morning (and sometimes into the afternoon).

The first few weeks on campus had a similar pattern until the 5th of November 2005. This was the moment when my world began to change. I wasn't a regular drinker both because of my faith and because I wasn't very interested in alcohol. I never really liked the taste. But this evening was different. It was John's birthday and he bought quite a few bottles of different alcoholic drinks. Just before I went to his room a young lady had offended me. I can't remember why but I remember being quite angry. I went to his room where some of the boys were playing Pro Evolution Soccer on Playstation and I picked up a drink. It tasted quite sweet and I began to take a liking to it. Before I knew it I had consumed more alcohol than I ever had in all my years and to say I was tipsy could be considered an understatement. I began to act rather crazy and was running around my block. I started a few fights with some people and then began to try it on with a girl that I had secretly had a small crush on (after that night it was no longer a secret). I punched a glass window and it smashed, and then I persisted to punch a wall and there was a 'pop' noise. Some of my friends eventually calmed me down and I was put to sleep.

The next day I woke up and had a look at my right hand which was rather swollen. I just assumed the swelling would go down and left it. A week would go past with my swelled hand becoming more and more painful. When I couldn't bare the pain anymore I walked to the local A & E in Hillingdon where they confirmed that I had in fact broken my hand in two places. As I had waited for nearly a week before coming to the hospital, muscle tissue had grown around the broken bones and my bones had settled out of place. The doctor injected my hand and went on to try to put my pinkie finger back into position. My hand was then plastered and I was told to come back the next week to see if it had settled back into shape. If it hadn't, I would have to have an operation. The next week I returned to the hospital and was told that my hand had unfortunately not improved and I needed to have an operation. Two pieces of metal were put in my hand during the operation, and I woke up to very intensive pain. I did what most young men would do once I woke up from the operation in such agony... I shed a tear, and called my mum. As soon as she heard that I was in hospital and had had an operation she had heard enough. Without waiting for more detail, she called her friend for a lift and came straight to the hospital to pick me up and take me home. When I got home my siblings asked me what had happened. Being too ashamed to tell anyone the truth I told them that I had landed on my hands whilst playing football. I doubt anyone really believed this, but as I was unhurt anywhere else I reckon they chose not to investigate further. I was spoilt for a week or so by my Mother, and remember having to shower with a plastic bag over my right arm to protect the cast. After a week I got really bored of just sitting around at home and returned to university.

It wasn't too long until I started to feel very frustrated about the whole situation. I was now at a point where I was unable to do many things as I was right handed and my whole right hand was plastered. During lectures I couldn't take notes, and was forced to take an exam where I struggled to write coherently. Depression began to creep in and eventually I got to a place where I felt quite lonely and isolated. My university experience which had begun with so much rebellion and excitement all of a sudden was the place where I felt at my lowest point. Eventually I got to a place where I was in my room by myself, and was on my knees crying out to God that I no longer wished to live. At that very moment I heard a voice deep within telling me that this was the exact place where I needed to be. It dawned on me that some of the greatest people that have lived, that I had admired, had also gotten to the place where they no longer wished to live. Where their will to carry on was based solely on a place where they denied their own selfish desires, and simply lived for others. At that moment in my room I decided that I would no longer live for myself, and instead I would live for others.

The next day I went to my university library, which at this point was still very foreign land to me, and picked out books about Black History and the Civil Rights movement in America. I read the first part of Malcolm X's biography, and also read about the likes of Marcus Garvey and prominent anti-slavery campaigners. Even in my school days I had an obsession with Martin Luther King Jnr's journey, and this was now rekindled at university. I started to think about what it was that I was going to do to make a difference, and discovered that many of the people that I was reading about used articles and newspapers to get their message out. I decided that I was going to do the same thing, and came up with a series of articles called 'The Power of Perception'. This was my message to the world about my new area of passion; equality. I wrote about the challenges that I saw with how particular ethnic groups are viewed in society, and how this was a problem that needed to be tackled. By the time I was preparing to write Part 2 of my new series the African & Caribbean Society (ACS) elections were approaching. All of my friends had now begun to see that I was becoming increasingly serious about learning and teaching, and that something had changed. I was no longer the same guy that they saw in Fresher's Week. I also decided that the natural next step for me was to run for the presidency of the ACS. Students on my campus needed to be given a different experience that went beyond the simple liberal atmosphere, and I wanted to help to bring the much needed change. When I told my friends that I had decided to run for President, some of them were quite against the idea. In their eyes, I was too good to run a society that was focused on throwing parties and seemed to have no passion for the personal development of their society members. The current President by this time had disappeared to start up his own business and there were accusations of corruption, amongst many other controversial matters within the society. When people said that my running for President may not be the best thing for me, I responded by quoting the famous words of Ghandi 'You must be the change you wish to see in the world.' My mind was made up, I was going to run for President, and I was going to use the society as the first step to changing the world from my university campus. My room became my campaign headquarters, and people that shared equal concerns about what was going on with the ACS would come and I would convince them to run for other society positions. The stage was now set and the elections were due to begin when the most unexpected thing happened to me...

The guys in my halls had gone to get food in the local supermarket and I was left resting in my room when I heard a knock on my window. My room was on the ground floor, which of course was not the best place to be if you live on a university campus in regards to privacy. It was a girl from my course who had come to say hello. By this time our block had developed a reputation for being a good place to chill out so this wasn't uncommon. I went to open the door for her to come in and the first thing she said as soon as she opened the door was like a verbal bomb being let off in my head. She said, 'You've got chicken pox.' What was I going to do? I had the elections all planned out, I was going for victory, and now there was an unexpected stumbling block. A lady called Abbey, who was like my surrogate older sister on campus, decided to call me an ambulance because I began to look very ill indeed. The ambulance came, checked me out, and instructed me to come to stay in the hospital overnight. As I was walking to the car park I saw one of the people that I was running against for the ACS Presidency putting up posters with his team. I decided that there was no way that I would leave campus to let them have an advantage, so I told the paramedics that I would no longer be going with them to the hospital. They made me sign a release form to say that it was my choice not to go to the hospital, and then I headed straight to the 24 hour computer centre to print some temporary posters. My friends were in shock as to what I was doing, but I was a man on a mission and nothing (not even chicken pox) was going to stop me. I put the posters up right next to my competitor's posters and went back to my room to rest. I went to the campus doctor the next day who confirmed that I did indeed have chicken pox, and I was instructed to stay in my room to avoid infecting anybody that may be pregnant. I couldn't go home this time as none of my siblings had ever had chicken pox, and so I was stuck in my room. I still wanted to run in the election, so I continued to put up my posters in the evening all over campus, and during the day those who could bear to see my spots and that had already had chicken pox would come to visit me.

A smear campaign had also begun with rumours that I was planning to cancel all the raves if I was to become President, and also one of my competition's reputation as an experienced rave coordinator becoming a key debate battle ground. Of course, I had no intention of engaging in such debates as it was certainly one of the topics I cared very little for. If I was going to win, it would be because more people on campus cared about their own personal development whilst at university than cared about who would be putting on raves. My argument was that there were many people that put on these activities outside of the society so there was no need for this to be something that was debated. It was a great political lesson about picking your battles. The show would still go on with or without the society focusing its efforts in this area. I was so focused on the election campaign that I seldom remembered that I was actually ill. It was only at the moments when I would make friends rub my back with camomile lotion or in the evenings when I was alone, that I would begin to itch and remember that I was in fact ill. I got a friend back home in Barnet to design an election poster for me, and this was one of the game changers. Of course this wasn't the 1930s but for the first time in the history of Brunel elections there was a coloured poster. I came out of my room in the evening, as was now the norm, and I put up this very attractive poster with my campaign mission statement 'Celebrating & Elevating a Positive Image of Ethnicity'. The next day the campus was buzzing, and I was receiving reports everywhere of how much people were impressed by my new campaign poster. This had changed the game. The competition tried to follow suit with their own coloured posters, but I had been the first mover and therefore benefited fully from this advantage.

After a few days it was time for the campaign presentations where each candidate would deliver their manifesto pledges followed by some questions from the audience. This was (and I believe still is) the most well attended political oriented event on campus. The whole of the student union had never managed to attract such crowds. The lecture room was full to the brim, and I had to stand outside in order to avoid giving anyone chicken pox. The various committee positions happened first, and then it was time for the Presidential candidates to deliver their pitches. I was up first, and was let into the room to great applause. Most people knew why I had to wait outside, but some people never and later told me they thought it was all a part of an act to make a grand entrance. I stood before the audience in a presidential manner, with a very dry throat, and a grey woolly hat to help to cover some of the spots. I had barely eaten in 7 days and was very frail at the time too, but I gave it everything I had. John had helped me to make my PowerPoint presentation, and also assisted in helping me to get the presentation onto the computer screen. I then began my presentation. I told the audience that if I was elected to be their President I would implement the mission statement 'Celebrating & Elevating a Positive Image of Ethnicity'. I told them that I would focus on making sure there was a balance of fun and educational activity in the society, and I told them that I would not cancel all the raves. My presentation went really well and I believe it was well received as I sat down to watch the other two presidential candidates. To my shock one of my competitors had created a video where he had filmed fellow students endorsing his campaign. The video was OK, but what was more shocking was that some of the people that had pledged support for me were on the video. I had been betrayed by fickle students. They later said that they were pressured into it, but it certainly made me less comfortable about the overall election results. After the presentations I went back to my room.

Voting was the next day, and by this time I had done all that I could to convince people to vote for me. The debating did not end however, as we now had to wait until after exams before we found out who had won. It felt like a long month and a half wait, and there were many rumours about who had won, and conspiracy theories about the rigging of votes. On May 14th 2006, at the annual African & Caribbean Society Ball, I was crowned Brunel ACS President 06/07. I became the leader of the largest African & Caribbean Society in the UK. I took over a society that had been famous for controversy, and was in financial difficulty. The society was one of the oldest of its kind, and had a bad reputation amongst its many stakeholders. With teary eyes I went to the front as it was announced that I had won, and I spoke from the heart as I told them that change would come. I gave glory to God and then the event came to an end. I told my new committee members, who were all very ecstatic about winning their positions; that work would begin tomorrow. Some were more pleased to hear that statement than others. I had already booked a library room for our first meeting in case I won. I was very focused on the task at hand and failure was not an option. I also realised the need to find a way to gain support from other cliques on campus and so I took it upon myself to create two new roles and invited two people to join my new committee who I knew would be allies that would help in the long term. I didn't know at the time that I was actually being very political with this strategy, but it certainly helped to get me a few extra supporters. I was being a leader that was bringing different groups together, and making sure that no one felt left out.

My first year of university was one with many highs and lows. It began with me battling to stay true to my faith in an environment that was full of various temptations. This led to me becoming quite active with the opposite sex, and also to me doing things that I had never done before. November 5th is a day I will forever remember as a turning point in my life. It was the incidents of that night which led to me remembering that I wanted to be significant in this world. It also made me realise that to want to live for others as opposed to for oneself is the best place to be. Writing became my outlet for communicating my ideas to the rest of the world, which ultimately led to me putting my name forward as a candidate to be the President of the largest society on campus, and the largest society of its type in the UK. This was my first real leadership role, and all the things that I had learnt before would now need to come in handy as I prepared for my second year at university. This time my year would begin as a President. We all moved out of campus a few days after the ACS Ball, and I moved back home with a sense of sadness. There was a sombre realisation that all the fun that was had in my first year at university would be unlikely to ever happen again.

Chapter 3

My Leadership Journey Begins

The summer of 2006 was spent planning for the year ahead as President. Very quickly I developed close allies within my team, and had an inner circle. The main players were one of my events coordinators, Stacy, and Jamal; my new Vice President. Jamal was a very interesting character, and at first I never knew whether or not I could trust him. This was because I had run against his close friend for the Presidency. After beating his friend, I wasn't too sure how Jamal would respond to being my number two. To my surprise he was very helpful from the start. His friend who I had defeated would also spend the summer starting his up his own business which I would let him present to students at our first event, and we would later become good friends too. Jamal and I were on the same course but never really spoke to each other during our first year at university. A few months before the election Jamal had been in a car crash where he almost lost his life. He was still in hospital during the election campaign, and his friend delivered a heartfelt speech for him in his absence. When he returned to campus during the exam period he was always smiling, even though it was very clear that he was in a state of recovery. His resolve to keep on going and to battle through such adversity was truly inspirational, and he remained someone that I looked up to throughout the year that we had as Vice President and President.

The summer saw a great deal of work, and my new inner circle was leading by example in preparation for the new academic year. I found a job as a student ambassador which never paid very well but gave me enough money to keep going. As we couldn't live in university halls of residence in our second year at Brunel, I agreed to move in with John, from my first year, together with another guy called Shaun. Shaun had become a good friend to us towards the end of the year, and I was quite keen to live with him as he was also a Christian. I thought that living with him would ensure I was better behaved than if we chose someone else who was more liberal.

We found a house round the corner from campus on a street called Dickens Avenue. We never looked too hard for the property; in fact we just took over a house that was being occupied by some students in the year above. The house had two double rooms and a single room, with the living room split in half by curtains to create an additional potential double room. John and Shaun argued over who would get which room, so I decided to be the humble one and took the strange makeshift double room that was part of the living room downstairs and we used the remaining single room for storage. I did feel a bit cheated to be honest but never had the appetite to argue. Once we had moved in I was able to focus my energies on working on the ACS. In order to continue my objective of getting my message out to the masses I also used the summer to research the best way to launch a magazine. It was going to be called 'Elevation Magazine' and would be distributed to societies across the country. I asked the media officer on my committee to work with me on the idea, and used a Microsoft Office template to attempt to create a business plan. I also pencilled in a date in November when I would organise an event that would bring together societies from across the UK.

During the summer we had developed a plan for the coming year, which wasn't something done by most other societies at the time. We also had a meeting in the middle of the summer where I made it very clear to my new committee that they did not have to like me. I said to them that if they stuck with me, we would be the best society the university had ever seen. We started to build our web presence, and sent out emails to old members in order to get them enthusiastic about the year ahead, which is exactly what happened. My leadership style at this point was very autocratic. I didn't want anything to go wrong, and I also knew that there were people on my committee that did not share the same values and ideas as me. Instead of spending time winning them over, I made sure that I was very hands on. I avoided conflict by making Jamal deal with any disciplinary issues that we were having. I believe in the world of politics Jamal would have been called 'Chief Whip'.

One of the biggest decisions that I made was to have our Homecoming event in the largest lecture theatre on campus. The Howell Theatre seated over 400 people, and was one of the lecture halls that actually charged societies a fee to use it. This was a brave decision as we would need to potentially double the attendance of last year's Homecoming event to justify spending the money, and to also ensure the room looked packed out. We took the risk and went into Fresher's Week knowing that we had to engage the 1st year students as well as the students in the year above as aggressively as possible in order to reach our target.

As was the custom, Fresher's Week began on a Sunday morning, and we started to approach students from the start. We had our own t-shirts on and were promoting our event as much as possible. We also had our traditional annual barbecue. I was very conscious that at the barbecue the previous year, my predecessor was busy eating chicken whilst his committee members were working very hard and they later resented him for that. I chose to do the opposite, and at one point I was actually clearing the rubbish off the floor. I served the food, and was as humble as I could be. The team followed suit and the barbecue was a great success. Eventually a member of my committee asked me to stop working and go to mingle with my new society members, which I felt was a sign that my desire to work hard for the team was recognised.

The barbecue was also a great success because we had managed to negotiate a deal with a local Caribbean restaurant that wanted to break into the university market. This restaurant had been unable to attract customers from Brunel's 14,000 students because there was a restaurant literally next door to them that was owned by a student at Brunel. We had initially tried to negotiate a deal with that student, but he was very complacent and believed that we would use him because he was from Brunel. It reminds me a bit of the Labour Party, in the sense that they almost feel they have a monopoly of particular voters no matter what, due to an assumed sense of loyalty. To his great shock, the student found out that we had chosen to use his competition because they offered a better deal (free food being the key part of the deal) and he decided to send a very long email expressing his discontent. By that time of course it was too late, and he came to the barbecue standing by the side with a very screwed up face and some flyers. After the barbecue everyone calmed down, and I was duly lobbied by fellow students to re-engage with this very complacent university student entrepreneur. I think he had realised by this time that I was not someone who could be pushed around and from that point on we enjoyed a civil and productive relationship. He agreed to sponsor our new t-shirts and hooded jumpers and all was well once again. Sometimes people call your bluff and you have to show them that you are passionate about getting the best outcomes for the group that you represent, regardless of whether it compromises relationships or not.

Wednesday had come and it was now time for our first official event, ACS Homecoming. This was not only my first event as President, but was actually the first event that I had ever overseen in my life, a fact that I must have forgotten at the time. A large queue began to congregate outside the Howell Theatre for the event whilst we were putting together last minute preparations and having sound checks for the performers. Just before the doors opened I got the committee to form a huddle and then said a few words to inspire the troops. We then opened the doors for the audience to enter the auditorium. The room was completely full, and the ACS Vice President from the year before was our warm up act. He introduced me to the stage, and I presented to the audience our mission for the year, Celebrating & Elevating a Positive Image of Ethnicity. I explained what it meant, what events we would do, and what to expect from us. We went on to have an amazing first event which was signed off with a performance from a dance group that was relatively well known within urban circles. They were called 'Flawless' and were the World Street Dance champions that would go on to do very well on the show Britain's Got Talent many years later. I had gone to primary school with one of the members of the dance crew which further helped us to get Flawless for a very good rate. The dancers really helped the event to end with a bang, and the next day we had to convert our good fortune into sales i.e. signing up members. This was the day of the annual Fresher's Fair, where we had to get as many first year students as possible on board. Membership equalled membership fees which equalled much needed money to fulfil our objectives. I developed a standardised pitch that I would give to everyone that looked remotely interested in joining. This saved me having to think too much on the spot. Some students in their second and third year of study also came to the fair and I had to adapt my sales pitch in order to sign them up too. A lot of them were very apprehensive about joining the society as they had bad experiences from previous years. I tried my best to convince them that this year would be different and managed to convince quite a few people to sign up. In many respects I still have to do the same thing today, only now it's for a polit-ical party that hasn't had the best relationship with partic-ular communities in the past. By the end of the day we had worked very hard as a team and had signed up a large number of people. We weren't given the final figures from the students union but we were quite confident that we had signed up members in record breaking style. Our Fresher's Week was now over and we could all now go home to rest... Some of the males on my committee took the opportunity to explore campus for some new female conquests. Being on the committee meant that they were already viewed as some of the cool guys on campus, and I guess they wanted to reap the benefits of this.

The next phase of the development of the society was to create a street team. This would be our eyes and ears on campus that would help to bridge the gap between the committee and the membership. They were also to be the ones that were important for effectively promoting our activities. These were our campaigners, our activists, our eyes and ears on the ground. Marsha was the committee member who oversaw the street team. She was an A grade student from her A-Level studies, and would carry on this record till she graduated. She was one of the most impressive people I had ever met and seemed always to exceed my expectations. I still hold her in very high regard, and as I write this she has already become an associate director within one of the largest investment banks in the world (still only 25yrs old). We agreed to reshape the old street team format, and to create a new 'senior street team' position where second and third year students were given positions in order to maintain a link with older students on campus. Traditionally ACS appealed only to the first year students on campus, and we wanted our year to be different. Marsha was also assisted by Isaac, one of the people that I put on the committee shortly after becoming President. Only one of Isaac's immediate friends had won a place on the committee, and he was a really nice guy who I thought would bring balance to the team. We had pretty high demand for our street team positions and had an assessment day where the applicants could ask me questions as well as perform a number of tasks that would show us who was best for the role. They got to ask me anything they wanted and I was able to explain to them the reasons behind why certain things were the way they were with the society. The hope was that they would then relay the message to the wider membership. They were also given further training around the society's mission statement. We were running the society like a very strong organisation, and were showing ourselves to be leaders in the making. Looking back, I think it was very audacious to take the idea of running a society so serious and I can certainly see that the experience helped to shape the lives of many of the people to this day who were with us back then.

I was very different from previous presidents as I wouldn't go to many other campus activities, and quickly developed a reputation for being antisocial. Some interpreted this as me being shy and others as me being a bit stuck up. I certainly didn't want to be known as stuck up so decided to work on being a bit friendlier. I was however always in my house, and seldom attended social events that were not my own society events. The inevitable female attention that comes as a result of being the President did come, and I tried to ignore it as much as possible. A girl once told me that a lot of the girls on campus had taken a liking to me because I was 'Nigerian, Christian, and focused'. I knew that people would use any of my actions as an excuse for gossip, and I did not want to have a reputation of being a promiscuous President so I was conscious to make sure there were boundaries as best I could. I seldom entered any halls of residence, certainly not on my own, and took the advice of my predecessor who suggested that I stay close to those who were my friends before I was President.

There was however a young lady that was a bit of an anomaly. She was a second year student as well, but had transferred over from another university where she had spent her first year. She was a cousin of the young lady that had identified my chicken pox in my first year, and so by default she was a part of our friendship circle. I met her at our ACS barbecue where she mentioned that she was a graphics designer. I needed some posters designed for our next events so invited her over to my house to help us do the designs. She was very talented, but seemed to be rather slow at the time so I thought it made sense for her to do her designing in my house where I could monitor her. She would use the desk in my room to do the work and would work through the night. Her accommodation hadn't been sorted out so she was sharing a room with her cousin, and eventually became someone that was sort of cohabiting with me.

We had a very peculiar association. Being true to my previous record, we started a relationship that lasted about two to three weeks before I realised that she wasn't the one for me. After we had broken up she continued to abide in my house (rent free) for the rest of that academic year. She would design the materials for the society and charged a nominal fee for her work. Rumours of course began to spread that she was my girlfriend, which suited me just fine as it meant that people would assume that I was with someone and therefore forward thinking females would give me some much desired space. This lady was a very big asset in more ways than one during the year. She would cook good food for me, would drive me back to Barnet when I needed to go home, and would design all of the material that I needed for my society. In exchange for this, she would of course get to stay in my house rent free. It was a very strange set up, and we would frequently both establish the fact that the association was mutually beneficial. I think she also liked the idea of people thinking that she was the first lady of the President, and a lot of my friends thought that she really had stronger feelings for me than I cared to notice.

We soon entered the busiest season of our ACS calendar, Black History Month. For the month of October, we would put on an event every week where we would celebrate varying aspects of black culture, whilst finding opportunities to educate the membership. Highlights of the week included a debate around my series of articles called 'The Power of Perception Debate'. Around 200 students attend this and it was very interactive and it would later act as a foundation for the annual nationwide debate tour that I was to co-found years later. The feedback was great. We also had a culture and fashion show where we got an up and coming comedian at the time called Eddie Kadi to host. Eddie was great, and we chose him because we knew that he did what was called 'clean comedy'. This meant that he didn't swear, was not blasphemous as far as we knew, and had jokes that were a bit more tasteful. He brought a fellow comedian along with him and they asked me if I would allow him a few minutes on the stage. I was a bit uncomfortable with this and it was decided not to let him on. This was because his jokes had not been screened and there was potential that he would say things that contradicted the values that I was trying to establish within the society. It was very difficult to have to be the bad guy, and very soon it became clear that this type of challenge was the first of many. There would be a number of similar situations during my time as President where we would have to discuss whether or not a potential act was in line with our core values. As a result, some of my committee members began to question some of my decisions.

Jamal would calm me down when I would have great feelings of hysteria, and I'd constantly get very stressed about what I would do next. Many nights I wouldn't sleep as I would be thinking about how to progress with the society. Black History Month eventually came to an end, and it was a success. It was now time to reduce the number of events that we were doing from once a week to bi-weekly. I was missing lectures to deal with society issues, and coursework was left till the last minute. My priority was the society; I needed to make it work and nothing else really mattered. The sacrifice was great but I was more concerned with enhancing the lives of the students that were on my campus.

I never used to visit other universities as I felt that my society was the best and it was the one that had the nationwide reputation at the time. Students from other universities would come for our events and come up to me after to moan about how their universities had nothing close to what we were doing. I was however invited to Queen Mary University to attend an event that they were putting on towards the end of October. I decided to go along with a few friends and stood at the back of the room. It was taking place in a kind of bar area with a stage and was hosted by a comedian called Kojo.

I had never seen Kojo perform before but was very aware of his reputation as a top comedian so was keen to hear him firsthand. The whole event seemed a little flat, and the President of Queen Mary ACS looked very upset and depressed.

I tried to give him a few words of encouragement when he went outside the room as I knew that many ACS Presidents across the country had similar experiences of having challenges within their committees. I never had problems nearly as bad as many other Presidents had and was in control most of the time. The event continued to drag on with a few performances, and then a lady came onto the stage to read a poem. She had short hair with some red highlights, and had quite a quirky dress sense. As she started her poem my eyes lit up for the first time that night. I was captivated by her there and then and thought that I needed to get her to come to perform at Brunel. I had already penciled in a date in November to do my first event where I would bring societies together from across the country. Ironically this was penciled in to be a poetry and jazz event. She made her way to the exit straight after her poem, and I did something I had never done in my life before... I chased after a girl! I ran and stopped her and told her that I was the President of the ACS at Brunel and I was doing an event. I must admit that I took a liking to her at that moment, but the only reason I was brave enough to approach her in this way was because I was doing an event so I had a reason to stop her. She was quite friendly and I think was quite taken aback by being approached by the President of the largest ACS in the country. I also dressed quite different from most of the other people with a smart shirt and jumper which she later told me caught her attention. I took her number and said that I would be in touch. This was the day that I met Barbara Soetan, also known as BEE (Benevolent Eclectic Energy) the Poet.

November was a new month with new challenges. We had to ensure that we maintained the momentum of the previous month whilst also making sure we did not do too much, I was conscious that my committee were students first and committee members second. They needed to do their university work and failure was not an option. Unfortunately some of my committee members were less proactive with their academic studies than others, those tended to be the ones that also caused me the most problems. I started to be a bit more flexible as a leader during November, and gave my committee more of a license to do things for themselves. I was quite apprehensive about doing this but felt that this was the best way to ensure that they felt part of the team. Besides, we had just had a great October and things were looking OK. Two of my committee members used this as an opportunity to put on an event themselves. They wanted to have a comedy night, and promoted this throughout the whole university. They seemed quite excited by the occasion, and I was happy to see them taking the initiative to put something on for our members. I still felt uneasy about the idea of comedians performing who had not been screened but let it happen anyway.

To my shock they had not booked any professional comedians, and instead handpicked 1st year students that they thought were funny. I came into the room and witnessed one of the worst attempts at comedy that I had ever seen. These so called 'aspiring' comedians were simply insulting members of the crowd (also known as our members) and making the audience very offended indeed. The event ended with people being very appalled by the situation, and I felt that all of the hard work that we had put into changing the perception of the society was now undone. I quickly went home feeling very upset and disappointed, and wrote an email to all of our members letting them know that this was in fact the work of a few members of my committee and it was not engineered by myself or the full committee. I wasn't very good with spelling and grammar so sent it to Stacy, a member of my inner circle, to look over. She was very down as she had heard what had happened, and was aware that the society had lost some support as a result. She had worked so hard over the previous months to help to build the ACS and was just as upset as I was. I felt let down by these committee members and chose to distance myself from the event as best as possible, whilst reiterating that we were also unhappy with the events of that day. The two committee members responsible also received the email as well and were quite upset too for being left in an isolated position. Although I did not mention names in the email, everyone knew who the culprits were and they were now outsiders in my committee.

If this had been mainstream politics, I'm sure there would have been a resignation or two at this point, but fortunately university societies are more forgiving. After a while I calmed down and realised that I needed to fix what seemed to be a committee that was falling apart. I met with the guys who had been involved and explained to them why I felt the need to send the message out to the society members, and I was very diplomatic about the situation. This was the lowest point of my time as President but I learnt a lot from the situation. I learnt that empowering doesn't always mean not being aware of everything that is happening and that you should always have quality control mechanisms in place. The fact that the leader should take responsibility for everything that happens is also something that really hit home, and I also learnt that there was a need to protect your team, even when they are in the wrong. Two wrongs never make a right.

This very turbulent week ended with the event that I had put in the diary way back in the summer. This was the event that I had dreamed would bring together societies from across the UK. I called it 'Elevation Poetry Night' and the strap line for the event was 'A Night for Networking'. It was on a Friday when many of the students from London had gone home for the weekend, so the turnout wasn't massive compared to our other events. It was also a poetry and jazz event so some students were probably quite apprehensive about what to expect. I had never been to a poetry or jazz night before so it was a first time for me too. It may not have been a large turnout by the Brunel ACS standards that I was used to, but for many of the poets in attendance it was an audience larger than anywhere they had performed before. We had about 200 people attend, and to my surprise students from universities across the country actually came. Barbara the poet also came, and this time I was even more captivated by her. I would watch her for most of the night and at any given chance would sit next to her and tell her a cheeky joke. She in turn would smile.

My sister Rebecca, who was in the year above me, came to the event too with some of her friends. She studied at Queen Mary like Barbara and offered her a lift back home after we had finished our poetry and jazz event. I made sure I told my sister that I had a crush on Barbara so that she could have a word with her on the journey back. She duly obliged and asked Barbara some questions. She said to Barbara something along the lines of 'do you go to church, because Sam is a very serious Christian?' She also strangely thought it wise to mention that I don't usually go for dark skin girls. Barbara now knew that I firmly had a crush on her, and we began to speak for hours on the phone night after night. The more that we spoke, the more I felt like for the first time ever I had met someone that not only understood me but was actually very similar to me. We shared a similar passion for good poetry and social justice, and also had a passion for making a difference as bold Christians. Our history was strangely also very similar, and our upbringings as young second generation Nigerians had a lot of parallels. Barbara was such a sweet girl and the only way I could describe her was like a soul mate. I asked her out on a date and made sure that I was very prepared. I organised for tickets to go on the London Eye, and bought her a box of Cadbury's Milk Tray chocolates. I was going to meet the woman of my dreams, and everything seemed to be picture perfect... until the day itself.

First we had been slightly late because I got lost on the way, and as a result we couldn't get onto the Eye. Secondly, Barbara seemed to be acting rather funnily. She would sit a bit weird and be very fidgety. I was a bit taken aback by the way that she was dressed too. It was all quite disappointing, and eventually I concluded in my head that this was just another one of those many occasions when I had thought that I liked a girl but actually she wasn't for me. After our date she sent me a message saying thank you, and that no one had ever done such a thing for her. This was in fact her first ever date and that was why she had behaved so strangely. By this time though the damage had already been done and I was now planning the best way to distance myself from her. Some would call this an exit strategy. She was about to go on her first international work trip to South Africa which gave me some time to think about what to do. Barbara had been selected to represent the UK at an international summit, and was going to be presenting policy recommendations on the world stage. As impressive as that was, for me it was a convenient opportunity to start to ignore her. She sent me a postcard from South Africa which I ignored, but strangely still have with me till this day. She tried to communicate with me via MSN messenger and also called and texted me many times upon her return from South Africa. I ignored all of her attempts to communicate with me in the hope that she would eventually stop trying. After a few weeks she did stop, and I believe the final message that she sent simply said that she would be grateful if I could at least let her know that I was OK.

The love affair with Barbara the poet came to end for good (or so I thought) and it was time for me to re-focus my energy on the tasks at hand. The society ended the year quietly and I had some time to think about what we would do during the second term. Students traditionally did not engage as much with activities in the second term as much as they did in the first. We had to find a way to keep the students coming, and decided to have a first event called 'Homecoming 2'. It was almost like a mid-term re-launch of the society and was an informal event with loads of Caribbean food; this time the food was from the restaurant owned by the Brunel student. I must say that the quality of his food was significantly better than his competitor. The new term would have a more chilled out mood to it, and events would be fewer and farther between. Soon after the term had started my next leadership challenge appeared, but this time I was far more prepared. One of the changes that I made to my committee when I became President was to reshape a role that I felt was going to give me particular problems as the year went on. Two people had been elected as the 'Rave Organisers' on the committee, and I felt like they would be redundant for most of the year if that was the only tasks that they were given. I decided to give them a larger portfolio and changed their title to 'Head of Arts'. This meant that they would now also focus on building the artistic section of the society, including a dance group and putting on the first ever full ACS theatre production. We managed to secure a former actor from East Enders to direct the play. This made the whole operation look very professional. It was all a very random way to run a society on campus and the audacity of some of the things we did back then still surprises me today. We had no fear and nothing seemed impossible. The challenge came about when it was time for me to read the final script of the play. To my great surprise there was much foul language within the play, and it was very abstract. It was one of the weirdest things that I had ever read and I had no idea how I was going to break this to my Head of Arts. The most confusing thing was how and why she felt like this was a suitable play that we as a society could even think of putting on.

It made me further realise that you cannot change everyone, even if you feel that the choices you are making are clearly for the best. Eventually I plucked up some courage and pulled the plug on the play. Not only did it offend the committee member who had worked so hard to put it together, but it also deeply offended many of the first year students that had dedicated their time to helping to put the play together through their various roles. Most of the committee understood that I had to make the call, but the next team meeting was certainly quite frosty. You could almost feel the tension in the air, and everyone was just waiting for the moment when I would be confronted about this decision. When the moment came, I ensured that I was very calm. I repeated my response as to why we had to change course. She eventually came round as I made a compromise which meant that she could bring in her old friend who was a drama director to start a new play.

Regrettably, we never did get to put on a production, but we did take people to the theatre to watch the Lion King. People would later come to me to thank me saying that they had never been to the theatre before. The next thing I had to

55

do was to find a way to appease the students that were part of the original play and were very angry. I agreed to meet with all of them and first listened to every question that they had and let them get their grievances off their chest. Once they had all had a chance to speak I answered every question honestly and directly and by the end of the meeting everyone felt better. The potential catastrophe had been avoided in advance, as opposed to having to find away to limit the damage afterwards as in the case of the comedy night the term before. People were grateful that I took time out to come to address their concerns, and I was happy that I was able to manage this leadership challenge much better than before. I was now becoming a more experienced and mature leader, and was looking forward to progressing further in terms of the things that I was now hoping to achieve.

The next step was to find a way to develop my idea of bringing together groups from universities across the UK in order to tackle inequalities when it came to employment. I had observed that a number of people in my university were finding it very difficult to get internships, and I assumed that this must be because of a missing link that was preventing certain types of people from realising their career ambitions. My conclusion was that we had to organise, just like those in the Civil Rights movement, in order to form a collective group that could really change things. So I began to sort out our next event. This time I would do a talent show as opposed to a poetry and jazz night. Universities would enter their most talented acts into the competition, and they would be allocated tickets to sell for the event. The proceeds from ticket sales would go towards paying my rent as by this time I had decided that working in retail wasn't an option that was for me. I had gotten a job with a DIY retailer called Wickes through John who was working there, but the feeling that I could be spending my time on more pressing activities far outweighed the money that I was receiving for heavy lifting, facing up aisles and sweeping floors. This meant that I needed to be very entrepreneurial on how I got money, and figured that events was the only thing that I knew how to do at that point.

So I progressed with the idea of putting on events outside ACS. My Vice President Jamal agreed to put on the talent show with me as a joint venture and we both invested a little bit of money to cover initial costs. As President of Brunel ACS it was pretty easy to contact the relevant stakeholders and we managed to prepare what seemed a very promising event. We started to sell tickets, and everything was coming together nicely. We brought back the dance crew Flawless for this event as well as some other acts that were well known at the time. This included an up and coming rapper called Bashy. I must admit that I never listened to most of the music that people my age did, so Jamal was really the person with the inside information in that respect. I listened to people like Frank Sinatra, and a lot of gospel. Modern day music never really did anything for me.

Around the same time I saw Barbara the poet at a friend's event where she was performing and I decided to give her a call as she had left before I could talk to her. Initially I think I had forgotten what had happened only a few months earlier, and soon after we spoke on MSN Messenger where we both never mentioned the incidents of a few months back. In fact it would be over 4 years later till we would actually bring up the episode. Barbara was one of the first people that I asked to join the team of what was going to be my new business venture. Putting my previous idea of starting up a magazine aside; I was planning on setting up a company called Elevation Networks and I thought that the best course of action would be to create a website where employers could post jobs for ethnic minority students. The talent show would be our first message to the world about what we were going to do and my room became my new campaign headquarters, similar to what happened during the time I was to run for President of the ACS. Barbara agreed to perform some poems at the talent show, and things seemed like they were taking shape.

The next decision that I had to make was what I was going

57

to do in the next academic year. Some society members had asked me to run again for the position of ACS President, but this was certainly not something I was keen to do at all. The experience had been very good but was far too much stress to consider doing again. Besides, people would probably have thought that I was attempting to become some strange sort of campus dictator who was trying to hold onto power indefinitely. Most of my peers on my course were applying for year-long work placements. It wasn't something that really appealed to me as I had very limited knowledge on what opportunities were out there and wanted to try my hand at entrepreneurship anyway.

Looking back, I reckon an internship of some sort within a political environment would have been great training for me, but there was no one to give me the advice that was needed for me to make the best decision. I do remember going to the careers advisor on campus at one point though and them telling me that my CV was very political. I eventually decided that I would run for a full time Students' Union position. The main reasons being that the Union had got in my way so many times when I was trying to do things with the ACS that I wanted to change it, and I also saw it as an opportunity to take on a position that was in line with my passions but wasn't too tasking. I chose to run for the position of Vice President Education & Welfare. I chose this role as I did not want to have the full responsibility of a President, and regarded being VP as an opportunity to develop a new set of skills as a number two.

A friend of mine called Martin was involved with the Students' Union, so I got his advice when drawing up a manifesto. I knew very little about what the Union actually did and this became very evident during the single election debate that took place. Thankfully not many students attended this so my poor performance lost me few votes. Voting was during the same week as my talent show and I was able to tell an audience of over 400 people that I was running in the Students' Union elections. They reacted with applause and I was quite confident that the work that I had done over the academic year would get me the victory. I would rely mainly on my reputation and the goodwill that I had built up. My poster was very attractive with a simple message 'Vote for a Passionate Voice'. I never had much more to say really as this was very new territory compared to what I was used to during the ACS elections.

I was running against the Students' Union Equality & Diversity Officer for the role and he was far more experienced than me in this world. I was worried by this a bit but remained very calm throughout the elections and barely broke a sweat campaigning. In fact, whilst many of the other candidates were in the Students' Union bar nervously waiting for the results once voting had ended; I went to have a nap in a friend's room on campus. I woke up and went to hear the results, and became the first ever student at Brunel University to win 1000 votes for a contested Students' Union seat. I had won the election because I had run the largest society on campus, was known for being someone with integrity, and had links to many of the other large interest groups on campus including the Hindu Society. My policies were clearly not the best, but my genuine desire to want to see people of all backgrounds and creeds succeed, as well as my ability to communicate with a diverse range of people, had won the day. Just like when I won the ACS election, I shed a tear to mark the victory. This was mainly because I had made my own Vice President, Jamal very proud and I could see in his eyes that he was so happy that I had opened a door for other students to follow in the years to come.

Students from the black community on campus seldom ran in Students' Union elections at this time and in that respect I was a bit of a trailblazer. People would now see that it was possible for them to run for and win such positions. We were now part of the ruling elite on campus, and the hope was that now some change for the better would come. It was also now very evident that groups that are marginalised in any environment have the ability to obtain power and influence if they desire to organise themselves for any common cause. It was the votes of the people who were disengaged from Union politics that gave me the victory in record breaking fashion, just like it was the students that were less concerned with raves that had given me the victory the year before. I honestly do not think that people voted for me simply because of my colour as I managed to attract votes from all sorts of people. They decided to vote for someone who had shown that he cared about the issues closest to them. In the following years, people from all backgrounds would win or lose Brunel Students' Union elections based on this same reason.

I finished the second year of university with great optimism for the year ahead, and was very happy to give up the title of ACS President at the annual Ball. I had learnt so many leadership lessons and fulfilled almost all that I set out to do when I had presented the mission statement of 'Celebrating & Elevating a Positive Image of Ethnicity' to the watching audience during the ACS elections in my first year. The Society wasn't perfect, but it had made some very evident progress and was left in a very strong financial position.

It was now up to someone else to continue the work that my team had begun, and it was time for me to push on in my objective of launching my company and making a difference to the lives of the people on my campus! One of the things that I experienced during this time was meeting the father of the late Damilola Taylor for the first time. Richard Taylor asked me to come to meet him in his offices. I did not know what to expect but I vividly remember entering the place and seeing all sorts of young people being given support. I never knew what the place was initially, but soon found out that it was part of a large industry called Welfare to Work.

Young people were being helped off benefits and into work, and Richard Taylor's office was right in the middle of one of the places where this was happening. Something told me that one day I would be a part of this world, helping to tackle the big challenge of improving career outcomes for young people. I was very inspired by meeting Richard Taylor, and still cannot quite imagine what kind of character is needed for parents like Richard to campaign on issues of youth violence after suffering such heartbreak themselves.

Chapter 4

Daring to Dream Big

The summer of 2007 kicked off with me focusing fully on my new business idea, Elevation Networks (EN). I planned to launch the company at a summer event similar to the previous poetry and talent show events that had been branded 'Elevation'. I decided to use the Holiday Inn in Kings Cross and had spoken to a friend whose mother was a caterer regarding supplying the food. To my surprise, pulling the whole event together proved difficult as I needed to raise sponsorship. I had approached a large investment bank, but had had no response. After speaking to a gentleman from my church who was working in the same bank, I decided to re-send the email, but only this time I re-worded it slightly in order to make it sound a bit stronger.

Within a day or so they replied my email saying that they would be keen to meet to see how the bank could be involved with my new initiative. By this time I had already begun induction training for my new Vice Presidential role and therefore could not attend the proposed meeting date. I felt that the strongest person on the team was Barbara and so I asked her to attend instead of me and gave her a brief outline as I had never been to a corporate meeting like this before.

Therefore it was Barbara who went to the first ever corporate meeting for Elevation Networks. The bank was very impressed with her and asked for a follow up meeting with us. This time they would bring along a marketing firm that they worked with. We agreed that we'd meet at the Pizza Express in Canary Wharf. The meeting was really good and they were once again very impressed by our ambition and asked for a full proposal. Of course, I had never written a proposal before for a corporate organisation, so once again Barbara was brought in to help to deal with the situation. Barbara and I met in my new Vice President's office on campus that summer and chiselled away at creating our first ever proposal. Looking back at it I think it was probably far more detailed than it needed to be but it helped to demonstrate how thorough we were with planning what we wanted to achieve.

Once we emailed over the proposal it was now time to wait for a decision on whether the investment bank would fund us or not. I carried on with the various National Union of Students (NUS) training courses that I was being sent on by my Union to prepare me for the new academic year and waited anxiously to hear the final verdict from the bank.

As the weeks dragged on I dropped them an email once in a while to see if they had made a final decision on whether to partner with us. At one point I got brave and told them that we were talking to other banks and that we needed to know whether or not they were still interested so we knew what next steps to take. This was me calling their bluff, we were indeed talking to some other banks but they were not quite as receptive. The extra pressure seemed to have worked however and I got a phone call from the Head of Diversity at the investment bank during an NUS training session that I was attending at Queen Mary University.

She confirmed that they had formal approval to sign a one year partnership with us worth around £25,000. This was brilliant news as we had initially contacted them for around £500. We had the disappointment of not being able to launch with a Ball because plans didn't go our way, but we now had an investment bank that would give us the much needed financial boost to help us push on. This also meant that we would now be launching at the global headquarters of an investment bank in Canary Wharf.

It was certainly far more than I ever imagined by this point and I was in very unfamiliar territory. We had to learn about how to deal with corporate organisations, and had to learn very quickly. The marketing company that came to the second meeting would help us to create our first website, and would help to create a new brand for the whole of the company.

Whilst they encouraged us to keep the company name, the marketing firm recommended that we change the logo and the slogan and came up with some ideas. Eventually we agreed on having the logo that is currently seen across the world today. It is shaped as a heart but has two chains that represents the corporate meeting the individual to form a connection. We also adopted a new slogan 'Know Who. Know How.' The slogan demonstrated in a youthful way how there is a need to know the right people in order to receive the right information on how to progress with your career. The company was now looking very professional and was ready to push on with its makeover. We entered into September with a wave of optimism, but of course I still had work to do as I was the Vice President Education & Welfare of the whole university student body at Brunel. I represented over 14,000 students and had to learn very quickly about what this meant.

Before I knew it the summer was over and it was now time to head back to campus for my third year at Brunel University, this time as the most influential undergraduate on campus. I was elected as VP aged 19 and all of the other full time elected officers were either postgraduate students or in the case of the President a recent graduate. People normally did not run for such positions in their second year at university, and even if they did it was less likely that they would actually win. It was a very big learning curve for me indeed, and it made me grow up much faster than I thought I needed to.

Fresher's Week 2007 came around, and once again I started the year with new objectives and a new role to play on campus. In my first year I was an ignorant Fresher, in my second year I was a society President, and now I was a Union officer. I had to engage with everyone and anyone, and I needed to take responsibility for the logistical aspects of moving thousands of young people onto campus, many of whom would not know how to deal with their new found freedom. I also had to help to oversee hundreds of upper year student volunteers who were called Contacts.

It was the Contacts' responsibility to support the First Years once they arrived on campus, but of course once the parents had left these same Contacts would be just as hard to control as many of the new students! There would be cases of over drinking, very forward males who wanted to have their wicked way with the new girls, and the campus simply would never sleep. I wasn't a night club goer, so some of the things I was witnessing were still quite outside of my comfort zone. Being a Union officer also meant that my personal profile had extended further to reach other audiences. My face was in every single room on campus through their student diaries and wall calendars, and I was given a t-shirt with my title at the back which I had to wear throughout the week. This also meant that there was of course new types of females that would take a liking to me.

When I ran ACS it was very much frowned upon to be a girl that engaged in any degree of promiscuity, or at least it was amongst the people that I hung around. It wasn't that many of the people within the Society did not do these things, but discreetness was the culture of the day. With this new audience, however, there was a larger sense of freedom and liberality. I guess in some senses this was a lot more honest as people would be quite open about their activities. It was like a notch up from what I experienced at East Barnet Sixth Form.

There was a particular female that was quite interested in coming back to my room. She kept on telling me to come and get her before I left at the end of the night. For me that was far too forward and a bit intimidating to be honest, so I took every opportunity to dodge her each day that this would happen. Eventually she got the hint and the next time I saw her she had a look on her face to suggest that she thought I was a very weird boy indeed. She probably couldn't understand how someone could reject such explicit offers of getting to know her. I was very happy by the time the week had come to an end, and went on to the next week as an officer helping to enhance the experiences of students on campus. Most of my friends had moved back home for their industrial placements year and so I was living on campus with postgraduate students who were friendly and very mature. I'd get visitors sometimes, but mostly I was by myself. I could have chosen to stay in the same halls as first year students but thought that this would be too much stress.

The 2007 academic year started well. I was working quite hard to do things a bit differently for the students on campus and was managing to engage some students with the Union who probably wouldn't have done so if I wasn't there. I was building relationships with the university and was helping to deliver some very important outcomes for students. I even managed to get a reduction in rents for people in a particular hall of residence because of some issues with where they were staying. A £10 discount a week certainly goes a long way, especially if you're an international fee paying student.

I was also managing to balance this with pushing ahead with my new start up organisation, Elevation Networks. Once we had finally signed the deal with the investment bank, work began on our new interactive website. We also had our first corporate event, which was a networking event for students interested in investment banking. The event was a great success, but looking back I'm surprised that we managed to pull it off. I certainly knew nothing about banking at the time, and if it wasn't for Jamal doing an internship in another investment bank at the time, we probably would have been very confused.

Jamal was on his industrial placement year and was learning a lot of new things within the operations department of Morgan Stanley. He was also trying to start up his own company that focused on development in Africa. He eventually decided to join Elevation Networks and became my number two just like he was during our time of running

ACS. We had a proven track record as a partnership, and also had different skills which meant that we had the potential to do great work. The one thing that had changed was that Jamal also had his own aspirations of running an organisation that would go very far. His vision went beyond being a deputy but for the time being at least he was happy to be a part of something that looked like it was going to grow very fast. My own view was that he would indeed go on to be a great success in his own right but what we were doing at Elevation Networks offered a good place for him to grow before he moved on to the next level.

By the end of October at Brunel my Union work really started to gather pace. By this time I believe I had my first ever full Council meeting. This was the highest governing Board of the University, and very wealthy and much experienced individuals from the British elite were Council members. They oversaw the strategic direction of the university and scrutinised the work of the universities management team. Some speculated that these individuals volunteered their time because they saw it as an extra-curricular activity that would help them to secure their respective elevations from Her Majesty or from Her Majesty's government, i.e. Honours or Peerages. The whole thing was all quite strange and often intimidating. The President of the Students' Union was a graduate, which technically meant that I was the only current student that sat on the Council at that time. There were moments that were amongst the most boring experiences I've ever had, as we'd sit down for hours and quite a few of the Council members seemed to have a sense of self importance. There were some people that felt the university should specialise and others who opposed this because of funding challenges that were predicted to come in the years ahead. We approved the university's £165 million strategic plan, and I'd regularly be lost when various large amounts of money were spoken about. There were countless times when I'd zone out completely despite my best efforts, however most of the times I'd pay attention out of fear that I could be asked to give the 'students' perspectives' at any moment.

When I was asked to contribute to these high level meetings I never disappointed. I was articulate and very precise about what I wanted to say. I avoided waffle, and certainly made sure anything I said was very short, sharp, and straight to the point. Most of the times I'd be briefed on the areas where I would be asked to contribute anyway and the university staff would come to the Union well before the meetings to lobby us for support on policy areas they were keen on. It was quite clear that anyone representing the voice of 14,000 students had a lot of clout and could push for things that staff probably couldn't. This also demonstrated the fact that many groups within society have little or no representation within power structures and as a result if anyone did end up being a genuinely legitimate representative, they would have far reaching influence. This was something that I would later reflect on during my political journey.

Council was one of many experiences as a Vice President that made me grow up very quickly. I sat on many different committees, including the Union's finance committee which allowed me to oversee a £2.1 million budget. I was also part of the team that oversaw the management of all of the Union staff, the bar and restaurant, and many other high level logistics. The first term was such a steep learning curve and it was a lot tougher than what I had experienced as ACS President. I felt isolated at times and the difference that I hoped to make seemed very often to get caught up in bureaucracy. It was clear that the managers in the Union had been around a lot longer than elected officers like me, and this made it very difficult to do the things that we wanted. The senior managers, who were in a sense our version of senior civil servants, would regularly block my plans and the wider support staff would regularly complain to me about them. This made for a very frustrating end to the first term as I was only doing some of the things I wanted to do. But it was all a very good learning curve and some things did get done.

To make things worse, I broke up with my then girlfriend towards the end of the first term too. We had known each other since my time at East Barnet School, the lady who had given me my first real kiss. Her name was Jane. I had bumped into her at a political rally that Reverend Jesse Jackson was speaking at in the summer of 2007. The American Civil Rights campaigner Jackson was attending the launch of a campaign called Equanomics. It was a very strange event and I didn't really understand what they were trying to achieve or how they were going to do it. It all seemed like a form of politics that was a bit radical to how I felt things should be done. To my disappointment they seemed to be the only set of people working on changing things from an equality prospective. There were not many alternatives in sight. I bumped into Jane and her eldest sister on the way out from the event and exchanged details. I asked her out soon after that and we became very close. She studied Politics at the London School of Economics and ticked the boxes of everything I thought I wanted in a girl. She was attractive, academically smart, was a devoted Christian, and had a passion for politics. She was also a Labour Party supporter, and had campaigned for a local MP in our area.

I still had no strong political affiliation at this point, although I wasn't too sure that I appreciated the Labour Party too much. I was warming up to the idea of being Conservative because I resonated with the values of the Party, however I wasn't quite sure about making such a bold decision. Jane and I would have regular debates where she would show great disgust to the fact that I was very pro business, and she could not seem to understand how I was trying to set up an organisation that focused on social change but would not support a government that seemed to think they were the solution to every social problem. She also struggled with how a Christian could possibly think the way that I was beginning to and regularly questioned my motives. Eventually we separated and I was very heart broken. She was someone I thought I was going to spend my life with as she had the things I'd always wanted in a partner.

Not too long after, I realised that us breaking up was probably the best thing for me. Her constant questioning and criticism had adversely affected my confidence, and to top things off she never really trusted me. I had spent far too much time trying to become what I was not and felt like I was constantly being compared to her accountant brother-in-law. My degree may have had an accountancy aspect to it, but I was far from being an accountant. I was entrepreneurial and was not someone who believed in job security first, social justice was my number one priority. Whilst she did admire the things I was doing, I think she found it all a bit intimidating and may have had a bit of a complex. I could never understand why this was the case as I held her in the highest regard. I must admit that I wasn't the perfect partner, and still had a lot of immaturities in regards to relationships. I clearly was not ready to be committed to someone back then. The whole situation taught me the importance of making sure you always make people feel comfortable around you, and to be conscious to show that you are indeed a human being and not too high and mighty. I could have made Jane feel more like a valuable part of a partnership. At the same time it was clear that I was still evolving my own world view and was under a lot of pressure for someone so young. It wasn't the right time for me to be with anyone as I was still maturing, if I was with anyone it certainly needed to be somebody that spoke positive words to my life. In the end it simply wasn't meant to be.

So I moved on and chose to use the heartbreak as motivation to work harder and push on further with my dreams. Any setback in my life would only be an opportunity to fight harder and stronger. I would never give up on the mission I had and decided to work even harder on Elevation Networks. Not too long after the breakup the first term ended and I decided to move back to my house in Barnet for the second half of the academic year. I found myself really missing home and my local area, and felt like it was time to go back. I rested and re-grouped, and prepared mentally to return for the second term.

One of the most defining moments of my time as Vice-President was an incident with the Metropolitan Police. I had gone to sleep on a Tuesday evening and woken up to havoc.

There had been a club night and after the event, two guys were involved in an altercation over a female student. A police officer, who was patrolling campus, tried to intervene by himself and eventually fell to the ground. At this point he called for backup and I was told that over 20 police cars descended on Brunel's campus area within minutes, bringing along police dogs and the like. Sirens were being heard across campus, and hundreds of students began to come out to see what all the noise was about. Groups of students began to congregate together in large crowds to defend against what they saw as an aggressive and over reactive response by the police.

Before we knew it, Brunel became a campus that was experiencing a riot. The police's aggressive nature was very intimidating, and as the majority of students at the club night were from an African Caribbean background, the police were seen to have been racist. As the night carried on, campus looked like a snapshot of the 1980s Brixton riots and students were arrested whilst some were bitten by police dogs and treated very aggressively. There were reports of punches being thrown by the police and the students, with people being injured. Both groups predictably blamed each other for these unacceptable scenes of violence.

By the time I had woken up, the challenge of dealing with the issue fell squarely on my shoulders. I was of course black, the former President of the African & Caribbean Society, and the Vice-President who oversaw welfare on campus. It was almost as if the whole situation had been written just for me. The welfare of students was indeed at risk and this situation needed to be dealt with very quickly. Students were very angry indeed, and for many of them this was the first time that they had witnessed things that they had only heard about from their parents and through history lessons. Some of the more passionate students arranged a march and demanded something be done. They also created a group on Facebook with a talented design student creating a 'Brunel Police Brutality' logo. The Police chose not to respond to their calls for 'justice', and it became evident to the students that any complaints would fall on death ears. They wanted to get the CCTV footage from the campus' security to demonstrate just how badly they had been treated, but the video had miraculously disappeared. Brunel was known as one of the most CCTV'd universities in Europe and for footage to have disappeared really added to the feelings of some form of cover-up happening on campus.

Eventually I agreed that a community meeting with the police and the students, who were very angry, would be the best way forward. I arranged the meeting and chaired it. I tried to be as objective as possible; I allowed the police to explain their side of the story, and I allowed the students to ask very tough questions. Eventually the meeting ended and peace was re-established. Relationships were not completely healed but there was a dialogue that allowed both groups to understand each other better. I left that meeting with a new understanding for what was meant by community relations, and realised that there were still very deep problems when it came to police relationships with particular communities. I also left feeling that simply opening up to have regular dialogue could potentially fix a lot of the problems that were still present, or at the very least could help to limit the possibility of very unwelcome clashes... also known as 'riots'.

The university did a great job in pretending that these events never happened and not before too long Brunel returned to relative normality. The issue with this of course was that the problems were not fully fixed but hidden. There should have been more dialogue, improved community engagement, and processes in place to avoid a repeat of what had happened. On reflection I honestly think that most of the stakeholders were not willing to sacrifice their time for better outcomes and would only re-engage if something further happened. This is indeed a problem I've identified with a lot of people; they are reactive not proactive within their communities. But I guess it's up to leaders to create those mechanisms and to encourage people to get more involved. As the saying goes, however, 'you can take the deer to the river, but you can't force it to drink the water'. Maybe

I could have done more, but at the same time I'm still not sure if I believe that leaders should take full responsibility for communities, any one person can only do so much. There is a sense of responsibility that seems to be lacking in many instances, possibly because people who are in charge promise too much.

Around this same period I met Pastor Nims Obunge. He was the head of an organisation called the Peace Alliance. They were formed in response to the increase in gun and knife crime and had managed to establish a whole week of peace that was supported by the Home Office, Mayor of London's Office, and the Metropolitan Police. He was one of the people working very hard to build community relations with the likes of the police and was often called into high level political meetings. I had bought a DVD with him speaking about politics a year or two before and finally meeting him was something that I knew would help me on my own personal journey.

We actually met at my church. I was leading a session with young men where I was talking about hope. When I looked through the window of the room I saw Pastor Nims walking into the church offices. It was very random, and I told the guys that I had wanted to meet him for years. They told me to go and ask him to come out but I didn't want to interrupt whatever meeting he was in. Eventually I told one of the Deacons in the church that I really wanted to meet him, and she brought him outside for me to speak to. We had a five minute conversation where I told him about what I was doing and how I've wanted to meet him for a while. He straight away asked what I was doing the next Wednesday morning and invited me to City Hall for a meeting that he was having. I stayed composed but of course I was in amazement at what had just happened. City Hall is where the Mayor of London presides. To be invited to a meeting there was something that was very far from my thoughts at that point.

I attended it and was very inspired by all of the very powerful people at the table that represented a wealth of institutions. Pastor Nims encouraged me to meet some of them to see if they'd support my work, which I found very encouraging. He quickly became one of my inspirations, and he would always support me when he could from that day on. He was the person that later put me in touch with a lady that was pivotal to my political journey after I finally made the choice of which political party to join.

Pastor Nims' and my own journey would remain connected for years to come. I began to support his youth engagement strategy for the annual Week of Peace which was very good experience. As well as our passion for politics, our shared Christian faith was also common ground that we would converse about. I had been a Christian for eight years by this time and was very keen to ensure that my faith was not sidelined but in fact was at the centre of who I was. I wanted to see justice and equality on earth partly because it was at the centre of the priorities of the faith that I had signed up to follow. It certainly wasn't easy being a Christian who experienced most of his work outside the four walls of a church, but people like Pastor Nims effectively paved the way and demonstrated that it was possible and was the right thing to do. So I kept on pushing forward, and kept on growing and learning what it was that I believed. This is something that everyone should always work out; their personal creed. It's what defines what you believe and what you will become as a consequence of that belief. I learnt that I believed that Jesus was the Son of God and that His priority was for us to reach heaven. In order to do this, we needed to confess with our mouth and believe in our heart that He was indeed the Son of God who died for our sins and rose again on the third day. That He is seated on the right hand of God and desires a relationship with every person on earth. As a Christian, I believe that our priority should be to love everyone regardless of their background, and to demonstrate grace and goodness to others. To defend those without a voice and to help those who are less privileged, something I see to be a mandate of my faith, and thus my personal creed.

Being Vice-President of a student union meant that I engaged very regularly with the National Union of Students

(NUS). I attended their conferences and also engaged with the National Executive and I attended many NUS training programmes. The whole experience was very educational and I was able to get a very good idea about the challenges that Higher Education students were facing across the country, and the policy areas that were high on the agenda in the political arena. I was also able to reflect on how my own university institution viewed things on the University's Council and how this contrasted with the views of the Union officials. This really helped me to appreciate better the many stakeholders who are involved in decision making and how it is very difficult to please everyone at times.

Most of the students were either affiliated to, or supporters of, the Labour Party. Anything but being a supporter of Labour was seen as high treason in many people's eyes, and in fact sometimes if you were actively involved with the Labour Party you could in fact be seen as right wing by the staunch socialists within the student movement. I found the whole thing very humorous and found myself laughing about how people within the NUS often conducted themselves. It was the only way of being able to bear it at times. I genuinely couldn't really engage with most of the way things were done and was not inspired at all by some of the anger they chose to use when articulating certain situations.

I remember seeing a particular man speak at an NUS conference. He was dressed completely in black with a baseball cap and looked like he had just been plucked from a 1960s Nation of Islam rally. I had never heard of him before, but shortly after I was made aware that he was an advisor to the then Mayor of London, Ken Livingstone. This person spoke with a combination of great expression and hate in his tongue. As a young person trying to navigate my way through this new world, I remember feeling so depressed about life once he had finished.

His suggestion was simply that every person in power was racist, and that racism would prevent black people from realising their potential. He never had solutions to his depressing analysis and the fact that he was in such an influential position worried me very much. Surely there needed to be a more positive solution-orientated approach to dealing with inequalities, and simple finger pointing would be very counter-productive. Some of my fellow union officers at Brunel soon decided to call me a Tory, and somehow it became a self-fulfilling prophecy.

On May 5th 2008 on my laptop at home in Barnet, I made the decision that I was going to become a member of the Conservative Party. This was for a range of reasons, the main being because it was the only political party that I had inner peace about joining. I knew that I would soon need to justify my choice to many people, and decided to focus on the values that I shared with the Conservatives (aka the Tories). This included the focus on family, enterprise culture, and individual responsibility. When I would tell my friends that I was Conservative they would first think that I was joking. Eventually they would realise that I wasn't and then the questions would come. A lot of people were very confused about how a black person with such passion for equality could side with a political party that had such a bad image and a negative history when it came to these types of issues. I knew that many people would initially question my own motives for such a decision. Some would indeed think that there was some form of pre-meditated desire to choose the Conservatives as they would embrace me as there weren't that many black people in the Party who were like me. This of course is an idea that many people have both inside and outside the Conservative Party when they see someone from a non-traditional background progressing through the ranks. The same thing seems to happen when we see women elevated within the Party. The reality is of course not that simple, and in later chapters you will hear about some of the challenges that I have faced.

After joining the Conservative party I carried on my work as Vice-President. Term ended shortly after and then I needed to help to handover to my successor. Stacy, who was my events coordinator when I was ACS President, ran successfully for my post as VP. Like most elections, the newly elected often feel like they will certainly do a better job than the incumbent. To be honest, I didn't doubt she would, as by this time I was disillusioned and ready to leave. Quite frankly I didn't rate my time in office at all, which is partly why I never ran for a second term. I was elected at 19 and my goal was to open the door for people like Stacy. I felt I had done a decent job, but like most sabbatical officers, I soon realised that one year was not enough time to deliver fundamental change. It takes a year just to realise how the whole operation works. The last action that I had to carry out after the handover was to deliver graduation speeches to the students who had completed their courses. Still being quite disorganised at the time, I ended up writing the speech in the morning of the graduation day, and used the same speech for both the Business School and the School of Information Systems.

I cannot remember ever being so scared before giving a talk in my life. The whole ceremony was very intimidating but it went well and the feedback was great. I did forget to address the Pro-Chancellor at the beginning of the first speech, a bit like one must address the Speaker of the House in Parliament. By the time I delivered the second speech in the afternoon I was much more confident, but still very nervous. It was such a proud moment to be able to deliver a speech to graduates. It was something very few people had the opportunity ever to do.

What made it more special was that at this time I was still an undergraduate student and really had no right to do such a thing. Indeed it was a privilege I'm sure I'll never forget. The speech ended with the words "and never forget; somebody, somewhere, is waiting for you to succeed, as it might just give them the permission to do so themselves. I'm so proud and inspired by you all. God bless, and good luck for the future".

I ended my time as Vice-President with great relief as I had certainly had enough of being a sabbatical officer. For someone so young and entrepreneurial, being told that I couldn't do things was very stifling and de-motivating. I needed to break free in order to do the things that I loved in order to make a difference, without people telling me things were not possible. I had learnt so much and had come to understand that change was indeed not an event but a process but I still wanted to break out and had no intention of running for a second year in office. My job was to show students on campus that it was possible to be from any background and to be able to win an election. In seeing people running for various posts after me, I knew that my one year had not been in vain. Stacy went on to become the first black female President of Brunel's Students Union a year later, and now I look at other students from various backgrounds years later who have run in these elections as part of my legacy. I knew that I would eventually go on to be involved in some expression of politics, but after I had finished at the Union all I wanted to do was to focus on becoming a successful entrepreneur with a social focus. A social entrepreneur! The next thing to do was finally to launch Elevation Networks and grow the business as fast as possible.

The Elevation Networks team had been reduced from 14 to 7 by the time we were due to launch, and I had offended many people by letting them go. The truth was that many people had joined the team because they were really keen to be a part of something that looked like it had a lot of promise. This wasn't a problem for me, but I was very concerned that many of the same people were not pulling their weight. Another issue with the team was that many of the people were very similar. I picked people that I felt had great leadership potential, but I eventually realised that teams need a variety of people, including those who are just team players. There can only ever really be one person in charge.

I met with a mentor called Professor King. He was a world renowned leadership consultant, and advised that I needed four types of people in my team: networkers, programme developers, administrators, and implementers. This was one of many leadership lessons I learnt from a number of mentors along the way.

We launched on July 7th 2008 in the global headquarters of our first corporate partner. The event was amazing, and we managed to get a number of important guests to attend including Levi Roots (Reggae Reggae Sauce owner and former Dragons Den contestant) and Wilfred Emmanuel Jones (The Black Farmer). We had a combination of students and professionals in the audience, which was in line with our philosophy of creating networking opportunities. Jamal opened the event, then I spoke to make the case for the work that we were doing. Barbara (the poet) was our head of campaigns at the time and she spoke excellently. Everyone was very amazed by the way that she composed herself on the stage and it added a real balance to the course of events. We ended the launch with a key note from Wilfred Emmanuel Jones. The night then went on to the networking part and people really appreciated what we had done. There were so many different companies in attendance and people saw that we were genuinely passionate about the work we were trying to do to tackle under-representation of certain groups within industries.

It was a fantastic experience, and I remember on the way home looking back to the tall building where we had just launched our company and reflecting on what we had just done. These were the things that dreams were made of; I had managed to lead a team to achieve something that we would never forget. We had met different organisations and people finally knew some of the things that we were trying to achieve, and we hoped from that moment on things would only get better and better. We went on to have an event focusing on helping to tackle diversity challenges within the fashion industry a month later. The event was done in partnership with a company that had far more experience within the entertainment industry called Cellar Door. They were run by older professionals, and Jamal's brother was one the organisation's heads. We learnt a lot from their professionalism and were able to put on a very classy event. It cost us over £7,000 to put on the whole event and we ended up making a very big loss because we couldn't secure sponsorship in time. We were so strapped for cash that we couldn't even afford to pay the company that supplied the catwalk for our fashion event and had to carry the very heavy stage flooring up several flights of stairs. It was all very humbling and we joked that we would never forget these moments when we made it big. The rest of the summer of 2008 was far quieter than we had hoped in terms of progress in the business but we were still hopeful that things would pick up and that we'd make progress.

This academic year had been the toughest yet but in a way it was the foundation of my own journey as a leader in many circles. It saw me be one of the leaders of a large union that had a turnover of more than £2 million, and as a result I was the only student to sit on the university's governing body. I was able to learn about how to manage an organisation that large, whilst also helping me to understand that there are many stakeholders involved when trying to make decisions within a political environment. Although I did not fully enjoy my experience as an elected union officer, it helped me to explore further what I truly believed and as a result I was able to decide where my politics belonged. It also allowed me to gain the skills to communicate with different types of people who had a variety of political ideas. This was also the year where a dream came true. I was able to launch a company in the global HQ of a leading investment bank, and was featured in the Canary Wharf Newspaper. From my days as a young man I had dreamt of the day when I would be involved in business, and this finally happened in a way that was bigger than I ever imagined. It gave me the confidence to push on and was an experience that helped me in the months and years after. I also experienced the highs and lows of a relationship and I learnt that I was clearly not ready at the time to be with someone, and when I was ready I would need to be very confident in who I was and what I stood for.

I guess the biggest lesson of them all was that I had learnt new things about leadership. How I needed to make sure a team had balance with different personalities and skills. It was also clear that there needed to be boundaries which included avoiding getting friends involved with the work that I was doing. Many of the people I had to let go from the team were my friends initially and took great offence in me letting them go. But I had to do what I thought was best for the organisation and from early on I knew that the vision that we had was more important than any person, including myself. I was older now, wiser, and more aware of what was required to become a success in a very competitive environment.

Jennifer, who had been the person within the investment bank that supported our work, told us at the end of the launch that she would be moving on to another investment bank. This was like a bombshell as we had done so much work with her over the year and there was now no guarantee that the investment bank would support us for another year. I guess this was the first news that really threw us and we quickly realised the one thing that is guaranteed within a corporate environment is change.

I went into the new academic year knowing that I needed to balance working on the company with my final academic year of study. I'd managed to get only a 2.2 in my second year and therefore I really needed to work hard to bring my grade up to at least a 2.1. I knew that one day I wanted to go into politics and having a low grade from a non Russell Group (top 20) university would only add more grease to what was already a very greasy pole. It was therefore time to knuckle down and to get very focused for my final academic year at Brunel.

Chapter 5

Preparing for the Future

Just before the start of my final undergraduate academic year a friend and I made a last minute decision to go on holiday. I knew doing this would mean me using the rest of the little money that I had saved, but it was something we wanted to do. The savings that I had from the remuneration I received from being Vice-President were now gone. This wasn't because I spent extravagantly, as by this time I was trying to apply a principle that I had learnt about saving at least 10 percent of my earnings each month.

There was an international student who I knew had accumulated very large arrears in the house where he stayed. International students do have things quite tough in many respects because they are charged larger fees and often come from countries where the currency is not as strong as the British pound. This means that money sent to them from abroad may not always be sufficient to supplement what they earn with any part time job. Of course they are also restricted in how many hours they can work whilst studying, and the assumption that all international students are wealthy back in their land of origin is often not true. Many come over because their parents know that receiving a degree from the UK can change their lives for the better and their parents make many sacrifices to make this happen. It is very strange to see how international students are treated when we consider that recent figures suggest that they contribute almost £3.3 billion to the UK economy.

When I heard about this particular individual's story, I was really touched and decided to clear my savings to help him get by. Hearing about good people that find themselves stuck in economic hardship is something that really gets to me and I knew that I could not help everyone on my own but was very keen to do what I could. I then chose to use the last of the money I had to enjoy a holiday, and opted for New York City. We spent five days there and every day was very different. My Mother's cousin lived in East Brooklyn so we had a place to stay for free. It was a nice looking area with really big roads and high rise buildings, but of course Brooklyn was known for not being the safest of places in New York. The excitement of staying in an area where we could sample the true culture of the city really added to the holiday. I've never liked trips where you are stuck in the city centre with other tourists and therefore never get an opportunity to experience the real culture. Some friends of ours that were also in the United States came to meet us so we ended up being a large group.

One of the highlights of the trip was when I visited the church of a gentleman called A R Bernard. His church was called the Christian Cultural Centre (CCC) and he had visited my own church in London before. A R Bernard's teaching style was one of the best I'd ever seen and I was very keen to visit his church now that I was in New York. Thankfully, and strangely, his church was literally a two minute walk from where we were staying.

To my shock none of my relatives attended his church, which was like having treasure next door but choosing not to go to get it, while people like me would travel far and wide just to get a sample. His church was amazing and the whole experience further made me feel like there was still a great place for Christian organisations and missions within society. The difference they were making in their community was exceptional and I could see why people like Hilary Clinton were known as regular attendees to the church. The service ran like clockwork and was so structured that it was almost like a show. The sermon was very engaging and when A R Bernard had ran out of time I couldn't believe it. I wasn't coming back next week as I'd be back in London so I was hoping that he would finish the message that day. To my disappointment when he ran out of time that was it. My learning from him would have to carry on via his YouTube videos and podcasts that I found on my return home. I told my friends all about him and I think that I probably helped to increase his UK fan base pretty significantly.

During the trip I also had the opportunity to go and visit one of Elevation Networks' UK competitors who were founded in New York. They were based in Wall Street, and I believe the same day that I went to visit them the investment bank Lehman Brothers famously went bust. Of course both incidents were unrelated but soon I realised that Lehman Brothers' downfall would have a ripple effect.

This was a defining moment for the world's economy and was the beginning of what we now know as the credit crunch. Unfortunately, this also meant that Elevation Networks would suffer in regards to its immediate growth prospects. Companies across England began to make redundancies and freeze employment and as a further consequence, diversity activities would also be cut, we had to think long and hard about what it was we were going to do next. We had already developed a business plan that was very focused on working with companies that had diversity high on their recruitment agenda. We wanted to target the big banks to raise much needed capital that would allow us to continue to work within industries where they had little to no budget to work with us. We could no longer do this once the credit crunch began to bite, and as a result my final year was a bit of a struggle. I spent a lot of time focusing on how to build Elevation Networks and many doors were well and truly being shut.

It did however give me the opportunity to focus on my academics, and my grades finally begun to look relatively respectable.

Jamal had returned for his final year also and he and I, along with another guy called Chris, Jamal's friend that I ran against to become ACS President, very quickly formed a close unit for the year. Whilst Jamal and I were working hard on building Elevation Networks, Chris was working on trying to find the best business idea that would allow him not to work for anyone once he graduated. He already had a start up called Elegance that focused on hair and beauty. He was still working on Elegance but also wanted to try his hands at other businesses. It meant that all three of us were chasing the entrepreneurial dream, and we'd regularly come into class very tired from activities the day before. We'd also regularly leave lessons very quickly to attend meetings and various other functions. But none of us wanted to fail at university and so there were times when we had to be very strict with whether or not we would take up an opportunity.

An example of this was when I was invited to meet the Prime Minister at the time, Gordon Brown. As a result of the work that I had done for the Peace Alliance I was invited to an exclusive reception at Downing Street with some award winners and other dignitaries. Receiving the invitation card for this through the post was very exciting indeed, but I had a lecture at the same time. I battled hard with whether or not I should miss my lecture to go to visit the Prime Minister and eventually decided that I was going to go to my lecture. Many people would later joke that I stood up the Prime Minister. The reason why my lecture was my first choice was simply principle: I believed that considering where I was in life and what I needed to achieve, a trip to Downing Street was less beneficial both in the short and long term to what I wanted to be or where I was going.

I honestly believed that the benefits of going to see Gordon Brown would be very limited to taking a picture with him at best and simply being able to speak about my experience via social media outlets at worst. I knew that there would be other people equally as keen to attend and therefore it wasn't something I needed to do. Besides, my thoughts were that I would probably be invited there again someday if I realised my ambition of creating a very powerful network that made a tangible difference. Of course, my support for the other political party helped further to reinforce the need for me to stay in my lecture. On a serious note though, I thought about the situation very hard before I made a final decision and asked people for advice. It was my determination to be someone that was led by conviction that inspired me then and still inspires me now. I once read an article where the CEO of the polling company YouGov, Stephan Shakespeare, advised that politicians 'downgrade conviction'. For me, it is the only thing that allows people to govern with a conscience at times and for that reason it remains a key part of how I make decisions.

Lectures at university became increasingly interesting. I wasn't sure if this was because I had now become a mature academic, if the lectures were actually better than in previous years, or if it was simply because I was attending lectures regularly enough to learn for the first time ever. Regardless of the underlining reason (which was probably all of the above), I was now really learning about business at a high level. All of the things that I had been doing during my time as Vice-President were suddenly becoming grounded within academic discourse. I was able to learn about people like Henry Porter who was a key contributor to strategic analysis. His 5 Forces model was something that I would go back to use on Elevation Networks.

I also learnt about things like resources and capabilities which really made me think about where the real productive assets within EN (resources) were and how we would be able to use this for competitive advantage (capabilities). The financial accounting aspect of the course was arguably the toughest aspect, but it also allowed me to learn about the various regulations that were needed to function as a business in the UK. It was all like a crash course in business start-up and was just what was needed to help me to understand better how to become a success in business.

There was a focus in the final year that was certainly not evident in first year for many of the students in our course. I remember a particular lady that was always in the library and I'd regularly check what she had learnt in order to make sure I wasn't too far behind. We had a number of courseworks to get through and the only way we would do it effectively would be through group learning and sharing of information that anyone had learnt or discovered. We also developed relationships with our lecturers and paid them regular visits to ask questions in order to get more insight into what was required to get a good grade. It was very clear that we needed to work smart in order to get good grades whilst chasing our entrepreneurial aspirations. This required us to make sure we could find things out that gave us the edge on our work.

Of course, I still needed to make money, and I wasn't working at the time. Elevation Networks wasn't making enough money to sustain me either and so the only alternative was to go back to doing what I knew how to do best; events. I had put on so many different types of events on campus by this time and so I knew exactly how to make something successful. The challenge was that by this time I was no longer a second year student or a union officer and so I couldn't do some of the things that I used to do.

My focus was now on business and so the only event that I could do had to be focused on this area. I also recognised that any event on campus that was going to be a success needed to be in association with a society on campus. This was because they were the groups with large constituents who were loyal and who regularly attended activities. I therefore decided to partner with the relatively new Entrepreneur Society on campus. They had been formed when I was ACS President by a young lady that I had put in charge of our enterprise activities. She went on to form the society but the first year or so was a bit rocky. They now had a new president who was a good friend of mine and they also had an ex-ACS committee of mine, Marsha, on their team. This combination of people would ensure that they went to a new level as a society, and the event I was planning on putting together would be the event that would be used to put them on the map.

The next thing that I needed was a headline speaker to draw a crowd. Entrepreneur Levi Roots was the outstanding choice. We'd seen him tell his story before and knew that he would add a lot of energy to the event. Levi had managed to secure funding on the BBC programme, Dragons Den, and was now worth millions through the selling of his Reggae Reggae sauce in supermarkets. He was from Brixton and had a very humble beginning and would add singing to his talks, which made his overall presentation more fun than most others. We managed to get him to come for free with us paying for his travel to Brunel and back. We later joked that we would have been better off being charged as the taxi we had to order from Brixton to Uxbridge and back again was expensive.

In addition to Levi we got one of our lecturers to speak. Professor Adrian Woods was one of the most inspirational members of the university faculty. His lectures were always very interactive and he would regularly challenge us to think outside the box. Jamal and I would also speak about our experiences from a student perspective, and finally we would get one of Jamal's mentors who specialised in internet start ups to complete the event.

Global Enterprise Week was in November so it made sense to put the event in the same week in order to raise its profile. Thankfully the event went really well but unfortunately we never raised the amount of money that we were hoping for. It was a great experience however and really showed us that there was a need for activities that supported students inter-ested in setting up their own businesses. I also met a young man at the event called Francis. He came up to me at the end and told me that he was a student at London South Bank University and that he was interested in establishing an entrepreneur society on his campus as well as starting up his own business. I gave him my card and told him that I was happy to meet with him to give him some advice. Francis would later be one of the young leaders within my inner circle.

With Elevation Networks, we were able to do one event during my first term of my final year at university. This was an event with IBM for people interested in working with the information systems industry. It wasn't one of our best events but it was a good learning curve and the event actually won an award. It won the Best Diversity Event at the annual Target Chances award ceremony. This was the first award that EN won and in the years to come we would get quite a few more for the work that we were doing.

So the first term of my final academic year ended with a whimper more than a bang, and I ended that year with a mood of deep reflection in regards to what I was going to do when I left university. By this time people also started to look to me for guidance in respect of what they should do with their lives and I began to mentor quite a few people. I spent some days in December meeting with young men and helping them to plan their year.

I combined all the knowledge on strategy that I learnt at university, through my time as a union officer, and through mentors that had given me a lot of useful tools. Combining all of this information with the knowledge I learnt through my faith, I was able to give very unique advice to these young people. The young men would in turn develop their own very strong plans and I would watch them light up as they managed to narrow their focus and know exactly what it was that they wanted to achieve for the year ahead. I also planned my year annually, usually beginning to reflect on this in December with the view to cementing my plans during the month of January. My life would be compacted into two pages. I had my Vision, Mission, with three to five strategic medium to long term goals on the first page. I then broke down these goals into steps, and the steps into actions in the second page. I learnt this from Steven K Scott, who wrote a book called "Mentored by a Millionaire".

I eventually chose to push on as an aspiring entrepreneur instead of finding a job when I graduated. My view was that one day I would leave business behind for a political career, but first I needed to have a credible track record of impacting my local community. I cannot remember how I felt once I made this decision, but later on in the year I wrote a note on Facebook which said:

"It might just be me, but now that university is over the ever echoing question is, 'so what are you going to be doing now?'

Living in England is very weird because whilst there are many options, in reality there are also many barriers... Some might say I want to do a Masters... but it costs money... I want to get into a profession but may not have the grades or it's very competitive. Others might think being an entrepreneur is just too big a risk, but at the same time you don't really want to work for anyone.

Whatever the paradox we may find ourselves in, one must appreciate that there is an answer to every question even if the answer... is a question (I'll leave you to chew on that). But today the answer I choose to take on is the FACT that IT'S GOING TO BE OK. King Solomon says 'Where there is life... there is hope'... Martin Luther King said in his last speech 'I've been to the mountain top'... David said 'though I walk through the valley of the shadow of death I shall fear no evil'... The great Rabbi Jesus said 'If you have faith as small as a mustard seed you can move a mountain'.

Tonight my heart is heavy as I can sympathise and relate to so many like myself in a place of contemplation of what the future holds... But I think a smile is needed.... Because regardless of what the future holds... We must thank God... That... we... still... have... a... future!! 'For a living Dog is BETTER than a dead lion'.... Ephesians 5:20"

Though I cannot remember all the feelings that I had when I wrote the above, I know that it was probably one of depression and sadness. I had a dream but there were so many times when it seemed like my labour was in vain. Meeting after meeting wouldn't materialise into any tangible deal, and money was certainly being hard to come by.

Soon after I finished studying the pressure was quickly put

on me by my parents as to what it was that I was going to do next. My Mother in particular was very keen for me to find a job so I could make a contribution to paying the bills at home. My Father was equally keen for me to get a job in the City as he felt like this would give me the experience to go back into business in the future. He didn't want me to make the same mistakes that he did whilst he was young, although he had studied to PhD level and had also chased the dream of being a great businessman. When he was my age he faced racism when he went for jobs in the UK and so setting up a business seemed the best option for someone with so many qualifications but with limited opportunities in Britain.

I was scared that I'd end up at an age when it was too late for me to change course if things never worked out and I'd have little to show for the dream that I was chasing. This is a fear that many young people with an entrepreneurial spirit are faced with when wanting to make that step into self-employment. For me, the answer was to continue growing my skills and experiences whilst trying to carve out some success in business. This would hopefully mean that if I ever did want to change course, I would have enough to show that I was employable and had the necessary skills. The next chapter will show some of the ways that I chose to achieve my goal.

Section 2:

Applying Principles

Chapter 6

Walking By Faith

It was 2009 and I was now a graduate, an aspiring entrepreneur, who had decided to focus on becoming a successful business man. My focus was on taking Elevation Networks international within three years. The challenge was how I would do this with limited finance and in an economic crisis that meant many of our target partners had frozen recruitment and spending in our area of work. We managed to secure some business with the Big 4 professional services firm, Ernst & Young (EY). They agreed for us to put on an event where we would attract undergraduates from ethnic communities that met their recruitment criteria.

The event would take place at the end of September so we had very little time to put something together (about three weeks I think). Hundreds of students applied to attend which was great, but a lot of the students applied when they were yet to receive their lecture timetables and as a result the turnout was good but not amazing. We sent EY a full evaluation and now had another large corporate on our list of organisations that we had worked with. This would be of significant importance when trying to engage the other Big 4 firms later down the line. It was also the last event that we did with my deputy Jamal on the team.

The whole summer had been quite turbulent for EN as we were not where we wanted to be, and now most of the team had graduated. We no longer had the safety net of being at university or on a placement year and thus it really was time to deliver. As the leader, everyone of course looked to me for answers which I did not have. I was also learning and was very much stepping into the unknown. We had a clear vision but things just weren't clicking. A combination of letting people go and people leaving meant that the team started to look very different from the original founding members, but I just had to keep going.

This was the toughest time that I had ever had leading Elevation Networks, and there were times when I was very low. As tough as it all was I think it was all a part of my leadership development. The hardest person to see go was Jamal. We had been a great partnerships for years by this time, both through ACS and then with Elevation Networks. Jamal was the most loyal confidant I had ever had. There were times when I felt very weak physically and mentally, but Jamal would be there to say a word of encouragement or to take over whilst I recovered.

The pressure from family and others because I had chosen not to get a job had meant that my health was also deteriorating. I would regularly have severe chest pains and would have to stay in bed for days for the pain to settle. The doctors identified the cause as stress and there wasn't much they could do to stop it. For a 21 year old, this sort of stress related chest issues was certainly not good at all. Jamal had defended me many times over the years and was definitely someone I looked up to at times even though he was my deputy. But with limited progress and him having his own ambition of progressing with his own organisation, our relationship began to be strained during the summer of 2009. I felt like he was spending a lot more time on his personal projects than on EN but I held back from mentioning it. I also felt that in many respects he had lost interest in the project but I felt like it was dangerous ground for me to confront him about the situation. He was someone who everyone knew had been very loyal to me and I wasn't sure how they would take any disagreement between us.

I think in many respects this was where I failed, as I did not confront the situation in a direct and honest manner, but instead allowed things to get out of hand. Things eventually got very bad as we both began to doubt each other's integrity, and in leadership you must have the support of your immediate deputy for things to work. Gordon Brown and Tony Blair come to mind. Of course this works the other way too, as a deputy needs to have the trust of his leader.

The breaking point was when a publication was released with the EN team showcased inside. We had a whole editorial on us and had even organised a photo shoot for the whole team to make sure everyone was included. Jamal was running late to the photo shoot however, and by the time the photographer had finished Jamal had just arrived. But the equipment had already been packed up because the photographer had to dash off for another job, so he took some quick photos of Jamal which he said he would integrate into the picture and we thought that everything was OK. The publication had very strict deadlines and was putting pressure on us for photos, so as soon as the pictures were received from the photographer I forwarded it straight to the publication's editor without even looking at the pictures.

About a month later we saw the publication and to our surprise the photographer had missed out Jamal. The editorial content of the interview that was part of the feature had also been edited and Jamal had been left out. He was very angry and went as far as calling the owner of the whole media company to ask about the publication. He also blamed me directly for the whole situation which was quite shocking as I had gone as far as paying for a photographer to come in to ensure the whole team felt like they were a part of this. I had also sent the draft of the editorial content to the whole team before it was sent back to the editor, so it was clear that the version that went to print was changed by the people that published the article.

Of course this is something that journalists do regularly so it would have been unproductive to complain, especially as the damage had now been done. I had learnt all the way back from my days running ACS that the leader shouldn't be seen as wanting to take all of the credit for things as it has the potential to create unnecessary division. I was equally angry at the whole situation but after a meeting with one of my mentors, I calmed down and humbled myself. I gave Jamal a call and apologised on my part for the situation and asked that we worked through things. He eventually calmed down and we arranged a meeting where he suggested changes that needed to happen for him to carry on in Elevation Networks. We left the meeting very civil but on the way home I felt very uneasy and gave him a call where I advised that it was probably best for him to move on.

My issue was that trust was no longer something that we both had for each other. Jamal making demands on what I should do as a leader in order for him to carry on being involved was something that I thought would open doors to me being undermined and it could spread as a poison to other members of the team. Too much damage had been done and it was therefore time for us to carry on our respective journeys separately. It was one of the toughest episodes of my leadership journey and meant that I had lost a good friend. We had been close to inseparable for the last 3 years by this time, and had grown to know each other better than other people within our immediate circle. In many respects we had become best friends and seemed to be on a similar journey in more ways than one. Our immaturities in our respective positions meant that we had damaged a very strong partnership. I tried to maintain the upmost integrity regarding the situation and never spoke about it to anyone in the team or outside of it, besides my mentors and girlfriend at the time.

Of course, losing my trusted business partner was something that many people would speculate about, and there were people who had their own ideas of what had happened. But I refused to engage with any gossip and never gave my own side of the story to people who were certainly keen to hear it.

The biggest lesson that I learnt from the situation was that leadership is all about relationship. I failed to maintain a good relationship with, arguably, the one person that I most needed to do so with at the time. Instead, I reverted to my then natural introverted self and let the relationship get to a place where I thought it was beyond repair. It was my fault, and something that I should have dealt with much earlier. A leader can never dodge ultimate responsibility. But it was now time to move on, and I needed to find a way to re-shape the now depleted team and to push forward.

I was very used to working with a number two and so I did not want to be very hasty about who it would be next. I had started a relationship in the summer with a lady called Bella. She had agreed to become my executive assistant so I had some support in that respect. We carried on trying to push the organisation forward and the team would all meet bi-weekly in the British Library in Kings Cross. We had about seven people on the team by this time, and this consisted of about three of the people who had originally launched Elevation Networks back in 2008.

We also had a young man called Jason. He was from Brunel and had a lot of energy. He was very close to Jamal, which I was conscious of, but was the only other male on the team who was left so I was very keen for him to stay. I wasn't quite sure how he took Jamal leaving but I always felt that I wanted him to give me a chance as a leader. I thought that I could help Jason to grow a lot more as he had such great potential.

In December I had a meeting with Barbara, the poet, where I agreed that she would double up as my number two and continue to work on the campaign that she had come up with. The campaign was called Visible Women and aimed to showcase leading women within traditionally male dominated work environments. This campaign was one of the only things bringing in money at the time so I was very keen for it to grow, and of course I could see the need and potential for such a campaign too. The team also included a lady called Sarah, who had been there from the start. Sarah was on my street team when I was ACS President and was one of the best street teamers back then. She was someone that bought into me first and the vision second, and as a result I knew that she was very loyal. Leaders always need people who buy into them as these are the people who will still be around when things don't seem to go the way that they were planned.

Elevation Networks was still taking shape and I was looking for the best way to make it financially sustainable and started to focus on engaging universities. Hertfordshire University's Enterprise Department approached us to source some speakers for one of their events and I began to do some research. I found a lady called Emma Harrison who was the founder of a company called A4e. They were a massive company that seemed to have the same objectives that we did in regards to tackling employment challenges. I did some research and found a London contact for the organisation and sent her an email. She responded to my message and we arranged to meet in one of A4e's offices. I went along and told her what it was we were doing and she was very impressed. She explained that A4e were currently bidding for something called Flexible New Deal Phase 2. This was the Labour government's latest response to helping to get people off benefits and back into work. The government would sign contracts with very large organisations like A4e that would be paid a fee, largely based on results, when they were able to get people off benefits and into work. The company were on the lookout for sub-contractors, which was where there was a huge potential for Elevation Networks to get involved.

It looked like we had finally found how we could make progress as an organisation. Being contracted by the government to deliver their 'welfare to work' provision looked like the key. I decided the plan was to engage with A4e and as many of the other large providers as possible in order to become official sub-contractors. We'd focus on graduates and unemployed young people in order to make ourselves look different from everyone else. I started to do research and after some time I had managed to negotiate five sub-contracts with these massive companies that were bidding for Flexible New Deal Phase 2.

Phase 1 was the first round which had happened before I was aware of this new world. The logic was simple, if these large companies, also known as prime contractors, won in

Phase 2, then we would win. This looked like the big break that we were looking for. I decided to go further and began to engage with policy from a youth employment prospective to see what else the government would be doing. Every time there was a budget being announced by the then Chancellor of the Exchequer (Alistair Darling MP) I'd look out for what they were doing to tackle this growing epidemic which was youth unemployment.

Alistair Darling announced a £1 billion pound fund to create 100,000 jobs. It was called the Future Jobs Fund and we needed to be part of the delivery of this. I wrote a bid and submitted it in partnership with the Peace Alliance, the organisation that was run by Pastor Nims. I knew that if the bid was rejected, we'd just write a stronger one with the feedback given. So when it was indeed rejected, we weren't too surprised. The next time, before we submitted a new bid for the Future Jobs Fund, I went to meet the team in the Ministry for London to make sure I knew exactly what was needed. To make sure the bid was as strong as possible; I chose to partner with the Youth Justice Board for England & Wales. This would be a major contract that would create jobs for many young people, including ex-offenders. The bid was for £650,000 and would take Elevation Networks flying to the next level.

So we now had a very large bid for the Future Jobs Fund and five sub-contracts for the Flexible New Deal and we were waiting for the results to be announced in early 2010. This was going to be our year, and all my efforts would finally pay off as we could now push on. Everything seemed to be going to plan, we had partnered with market leaders and had received advice directly from the people that would decide who won these contracts. We could be turning over in excess of £1 million by the end of the next financial year; the magic number for any entrepreneur. But the one final thing that had to go our way was also the one thing that I probably didn't really want to happen... Labour would have to win the 2010 general elections. For if the Conservative Party won in 2010 they might scrap the Future Jobs Fund and promised to replace the Flexible New Deal with a remodelled Work Programme that was very different to what we had been subcontracted to do. My ideal outcome would be that the Conservatives did win but either all the contracts would be issued before the elections or that the Conservatives would do what most people think politicians do and fail to deliver on their promise.

Unfortunately both of my ideal outcomes never happened and we were instead faced with arguably the worst case scenario. The Conservatives, who I had campaigned for that year, formed a coalition having failed to win a majority in Parliament. Within the first six days of the coalition taking office, the new Chancellor George Osborne MP released an emergency budget where he announced that he would be scrapping the Future Jobs Fund, effective immediately with no replacement. The government would also be cancelling all tenders for the Flexible New Deal and would be releasing details about their new Work Programme at a later date.

I had put all of my focus and efforts on securing these contracts. I had managed to get into contact with some of the largest companies in the country and had negotiated very promising deals. I became an expert within the youth employment world within a matter of months and was looking forward to making a big difference. But within days I was now back to square one. How could I explain this to my team who were all very excited about this next level which was being promised for months and where would we go from here? This was certainly a very low point in my business journey. I guess a lesson to anyone reading this would be to never hedge your bets on public finance. A shift in any policy area could mean you going out of business if you relied solely on a government for growth. I'd also say that in business you must have multiple sources of income to avoid suffering from any changes in demand, and the final lesson would be to be able to adapt very quickly. This is what I had to do with Elevation Networks to an extent, as of course I wasn't ready to give up.

We went into the summer of 2010 with our focus now on how we could penetrate the schools market. The first way we wanted to do this was through the provision of summer schemes. We managed to get some money from my church to put on a scheme in Barnet. Sarah from the EN team had extensive experience from her work with various education focused organisations and designed an innovative programme that would help to change the lives of the young people on the course.

We called the course Elevate Your Future and the theme for the first year would be enterprise. The young people would be taught various business tools whilst also being involved in activities that would challenge their mindset. They would be put into groups and have to develop a business idea that would be pitched to a panel of experts. The vision was to have a summer scheme in every borough across London, so Barnet was very much the pilot. I was the lead facilitator for the scheme as I wanted to see if the course material was good enough to be rolled out. I also used my personal contacts within some of the highest offices in London to ensure we gave the young people an experience that they'd never forget. We visited City Hall where we got the young people to meet one of the Deputy Mayors of London and also went to HSBC's Headquarters in Canary Wharf which is one of the tallest buildings in the UK. The young people also went to visit a local academy where I explained the politics behind these types of schools, and they were driven along one of the wealthiest roads in the country; Bishops Avenue.

We exposed the young people to things that many adults would never have the opportunity to experience, and they met some highly influential people. This was Elevation Networks delivering a programme with the underlining philosophy of networking at its core. The course ended with them pitching their business ideas to a panel that included a local councillor, a business man, and someone from the community action team in my church. The winners and runners up were given seed funding to progress their idea, and all of the young people were given a certificate of achievement for completing the course. We had created a course that was designed to expose young people from under-represented backgrounds to the many career possibilities using entrepreneurship as the underlining theme. Today, so many of those young people have gone on to achieve great things and are either in Higher Education or continuing their studying in school or college.

I decided that I wouldn't give up on being a part of the delivery of the public service response to youth unemployment. We were a youth led organisation with much to offer. So work began on making sure we secured a contract under the new Work Programme. This was a lot tougher than Flexible New Deal as the overall contracts were larger but more emphasis was placed on payment by results. As a consequence of this the larger companies were less willing to use our services as subcontractors because it would mean them spending more money when they were being given much less cash upfront from the government. Some of these large contractors, who were known as primes, would agree to put us into their bids but would not guarantee any volumes in regards to how many people we would work with per year. The fear was that a lot of the primes would simply be putting organisations like our own in their bids to make them sound as good as possible. They would then not use us for the overall delivery and could not face any legal challenge as they had not stated any volumes or fixed prices during the negotiation period.

We secured two subcontracts from bids that had been successful during the tendering period, however just like we had predicted the primes were very slow in engaging subcontractors like ourselves. Community organisations were now at a place where they were very involved in these sorts of activities under Labour, but the new Big Society philosophy under the coalition had not created more opportunities for their engagement. This was of course a great paradox because the very nature of the message from the Conservative led government was that communities, charities, social enterprises, and well meaning people could participate in getting Britain back to being great.

Unfortunately it seemed that the government had negotiated contracts that created the opposite situation. Large primes feared that they would not win contracts if they priced their work too high, and therefore had to use underhanded tactics falsely to partner with the companies that were smaller in order to ensure they still seemed to be engaging with the new so called Big Society's community agenda. Elevation Networks would be one of the companies that felt the impact of these changes, but thankfully by this time we had already learnt that you should not rely solely on public sector contracts to be a sustainable going concern. For many of these prime contractors however, public finance was their only source of income.

From an ethical perspective, I question just how valuable such arrangements are for the general public. Some firms have been known to make excessive profits from large government contracts, and have compromised on overall quality. I'd be more comfortable if not-for-profit organisations were more involved in delivering the majority of the nation's services, and more jobs were created instead of large profits. I also think that social enterprises must be a better way forward, and that the government should find better ways of ensuring large government contractors are engaging community groups in more significant ways than they are currently. Price should never be the most important determining factor when it comes to the delivery of public services.

Business was finally beginning to pick up towards the end of 2010. We had managed to coordinate the largest ever debate tour targeting African & Caribbean Societies across the UK. Whilst in a meeting with Francis, the young man from London Southbank University, he mentioned that he wanted to do a tour of universities with motivational speakers. I told him that any tour would need to have a stronger theme to gain mass appeal. We then came up with the idea of a debate tour, and took the concept for branding from a film starring

Denzel Washington called "The Great Debaters". The film was based on students who debated in a national championship during the Civil Rights Movement.

Our vision was to inspire the next generation of voters to get involved in politics and to recognise that they do have opinions that can contribute to nationwide debates. Since meeting Francis in 2008, he had become a mentee of mine and was doing great things. He had also joined Elevation Networks team by this point as well as pursuing his own business venture. By this time we had developed a very strong partnership with another Big 4 organisation, Deloitte LLP, and would eventually win an award with them for the partnership. We were also working very effectively with the Youth Justice Board for England and Wales, and had actually appointed one of their board members as our own board chairman. He was a former school head teacher with great experience that was relevant to the work that we were trying to do. We began to diversify the types of industries that we were collaborating with and were now doing work in technology, politics, PR, fashion, banking, and others. We also had our first offices by this time and were based in 1 London Bridge. The prime location was chosen because it meant that we would be in the centre of the places where companies we wished to work with were. We spent quite a lot of money on the office rent, which meant that no one could take a wage at this point, but I felt it was in the interest of the long term vision of the company. We also started to apply for grants and were fortunate to win cash from the Evening Standard's Dispossessed Fund for our work with long term unemployed young people. Our membership was growing with the core team now having 8 people and over 70 volunteers across the UK were supporting our work. The organisation was now at the place where we had a stronger model and a track record of successes to use when attempting to win business. The foundations were now set for Elevation Networks to push on. We certainly weren't where we wanted to be, but I felt that a tipping point would be just around the corner.

As 2010 ended I began to feel a strong pull towards politics. Stronger than maybe I'd ever had before, and I decided that in 2011 I would stop running Elevation Networks on a day to day basis, and would instead serve as a board member. I also felt like I could not take the organisation any further and it was time for someone else with different skills to complete the work that I had begun on my university campus all those years ago. We announced to our members that I would be stepping aside from my role as CEO and from April 1st 2011 would no longer run the organisation full time. Instead, I would chase my dream of making a difference to people's lives on a policy level, and would continue to support Elevation Networks as a board member.

All that I had seen and experienced over the years had led me to believe that I could help to represent communities that were marginalised and traditionally less represented within the political world. The new Chief Executive would be Barbara Soetan aka Barbara the poet. She was the outstanding candidate because she had great skill and by this time was not the same girl that I met at Queen Mary University. She had now worked in 9 countries, met 6 heads of state, and won various awards for her work. She was the 2008 UK Young Activist of the year and her experiences ranged from being a UN observer at the 2008 Kenyan elections to facilitating peace talks between North and South Cyprus. She was an amazingly well skilled and inspirational young lady, but perhaps more important than all of this, she had stayed with Elevation Networks and supported the vision from the start. She was by now the only remaining team member that was there from the beginning. As for me, I never knew what the future would hold but I did know that I had unfinished business in the world of enterprise. I had done reasonably well with Elevation Networks, taking it from simply being a dream to being an award winning social enterprise that had worked with over 32 organisations and engaged thousands of young people across the country. But I knew that I still desired greater success in business and didn't know where this would come from. My focus was now politics, but I'd regularly state that business was a close cousin of politics and so I really wanted to be able to say I had a mature relationship with both.

I continued to be heavily involved in the overall strategic direction of EN but was careful not to step in to lead and was conscious of the fact that Barbara needed to be able to do things her own way. We would regularly discuss where the organisation needed to go and I would still act as an ambassador for the company, as by this time my public profile was increasing steadily. I still wrote many of the bids for the organisation, and Barbara still needed to complete one of her part time contracts so it took a few months before she could take over the running of the organisation fully. EN is now being run very smoothly by Barbara and is growing steadily under Barbara's leadership in its London offices.

I continued to do whatever I could as a board member, and of course one can never stop being the founder of something. I've also sat on various other boards including one of the 2012 Olympics committee engagement boards. The most high profile of my board membership is with the Peace Alliance. Following the death of Mark Duggan, riots broke out in Tottenham and the Peace Alliance was a key part in helping to deal with tensions within the community. The organisation has also recently taken over the £2.4 million newly refurbished Tottenham Town Hall and continues to work hard in tackling issues such as gun and knife crime in England's capital. It is certainly quite inspiring to be now the youngest board member of the Peace Alliance considering how I met the chief executive, Pastor Nims, all those years ago. In addition to this, I am now co-chairman of the Spirit of London Awards Select Committee, helping to grow what is the largest youth award ceremony in the UK.

I also spent a little while on the management team of another organisation. The organisation was identified as the fastest growing social enterprise in Britain, going from a turnover of £180,000 to £1.2 million in a year. Ironically their high growth was a result of their success with the Future Jobs Fund. They were now struggling because they were too heavily reliant on this fund before it was cut and were now looking for ways to diversify their income streams. I helped them to secure a new government subcontract with a large company called G4S, as well as a corporate partnership with a financial services firm. After this I decided that it was time for me to move on. It was the first time that I had worked for someone in such a capacity, and I felt very stifled and under-utilised. I don't think that the issue was that I was working for someone else, but it was that I never felt like I was growing and also felt like the organisation was in need of some changes very quickly. I never had to give a long notice period before I moved on as I hadn't been there for too long anyway, however they certainly were not happy with the situation. Within a week of me leaving I was made aware that the founder who had been away during my time there had returned and was now implementing the much needed changes to the organisation that I had felt were needed. I learnt a lot from my short time there and once again realised that it was very important to have a diversity of income streams as a business. This seemed to be the underlining lesson that I was learning whenever things hadn't gone too well. I have certainly learnt quite a bit through my experiences in business. The first thing I would say that I have learnt is the importance of having a unique set of personal skills. Time and time again I saw young people that were not as bright as their competitors but had technical skills that allowed them to progress further when trying to obtain finance for setting up an enterprise. Technical skills combined with an entrepreneurial spirit seem to be what will continue to win the day as the world becomes more global and more technological. Everybody wants to fund the next Microsoft or Facebook; very few people want to fund things that are service driven without a strong unique selling point. I'd encourage young business hopefuls to study a technical skill like Information Technology, Engineering or Accounting. It may well be tough in the first instance but will mean that you have something that is in demand and valuable to the world at large.

The other thing that I've learnt is that leadership is the core skill that is needed to take an organisation to the next level. The leader is the most important person on the team and if they are not on the ball the organisation will inevitably suffer. I saw this first with myself, and then learnt this from many of the other leaders that I've either worked with or been advised by. Good leaders are able to create a strong team that is always improving with a very low staff turnover in most instances.

When I first started to run Elevation Networks I would regularly let go and/ or lose staff members. This was not good for morale as people feared that they would be the next to go. It certainly wasn't good for the growth of the organisation and really slowed things down as I'd need to find replacements. A business needs a team that is dedicated to the cause and talented enough to bring things to fruition. The team must also have a lot of variety to it. You need good networkers, good product developers, good administrators, and strong implementers. If everyone is a networker on your team you'll be stuck with a bunch of people that just want to be out there but don't want to do any implementation work. If everyone on the team is just good at building programmes or products, no one will specialise in bringing the money in, and if everyone is a doer they'll be no thinkers. Variety is literally the spice of life when attempting to build and effectively lead a team. This is something that was a big problem in the early days of EN. I picked excellent people that all had very similar characteristics to me. Many of them were great leaders within their own right, when I should have really selected some people that were also really good at admin or developing.

Business is always about adding value to someone or something. I learnt that you must have a buyer and a seller for a business to work. This may sound simple, but many times when people are entrepreneurial with a social conscience they forget this fact. There has been way too many times when I've met aspiring entrepreneurs who have come to me with their dream to tackle a big problem but the product is not clear or they have not identified a credible income stream.

This was the problem that Elevation Networks had when it first started. We wanted to help make young people from under-represented groups more competitive in the labour market. This was a very clear mission but how it translated into a credible going concern was something that took us a very long time to find out. Whilst we were still trying to understand this, some companies that had begun around the same time as us were flying high and generating profits beyond anything we could have imagined. It is also important to partner continuously and effectively with organisations and people at a higher level than you. This makes you grow a lot faster and adds a lot more credibility to you going forward.

Elevation Networks has worked with major brands including the BBC, IBM, Barclays, HSBC, Standard Bank, Deloitte, Ernst & Young and many others over its brief existence. This means when the organisation is pitching its services the team can say 'we've done all of this work with these people, this shows that we have some value'. We may have failed to progress initially with the government contracting, but it was certainly a valuable experience. It gave us the knowledge that allowed us to go again, and now Elevation Networks is delivering on a number of local and national government contracts. Above all, the ethos of being highly courageous and never giving up is what separates winners from losers. I always dreamt big when it came to Elevation Networks and was courageous enough to negotiate contracts with big government contractors that turned over millions, and sometimes billions, of pounds. I tell myself that we never won those initial contracts because it simply wasn't meant to be. It wasn't yet our time to push on; we still had a lot more things to learn before we made it big. Who knows, if Gordon Brown had won the 2010 election, we may have made a lot of money in the short term, but in the medium to long term Labour's refusal to deal with the public finances earlier would have meant we could have suffered.

I guess one could argue that I've had very interesting business experience to date. As I write this I am 24 years of age and some would argue that it hasn't been too bad a return, but I certainly desire to do a lot more, sooner rather than later, and continue to have my eye out for good opportunities.

Shortly after I stood down as CEO Elevation Networks I was watching Sky News and there was a gentleman being interviewed about a new organisation that he had started up. It was called the New Entrepreneurs Foundation, and they were looking for the top 25 young entrepreneurs in the country who they would pair up with a top business man to work with for one year. I thought this was just what I needed so I went onto their website and applied. To my surprise there were four stages of the selection process which included two interviews at an assessment centre and a psychometric test. I had never applied for a job like this before so this was all very intimidating but I thought I'd go for it anyway. I was indeed selected as one of their top candidates and the feedback was excellent. It was now time for them to pair me up with an entrepreneur. I visited a private investment firm in Mayfair and met an entrepreneur that I found quite stale to be honest. He had had such great editorials written about him in various newspapers, which just goes to show you shouldn't believe everything that you read in papers. He was looking for an administrator really and I wasn't sure that I would last there. We didn't hit it off which was surprising because we both ran networks and arguably had pretty strong communication skills. He was probably the one that was less skilful in my opinion as I could see many of the various techniques that he used to win with people.

I was then sent to meet a Conservative Party entrepreneur. He was the co-founder of a leading polling company. I read his story and was very inspired by it. He had in fact ran for a seat in Parliament some years back. I went along to meet him but I was first met by his strategy coordinator. He came in afterwards and I thought everything had gone quite well. But to my surprise I was told that they would like to interview me for a second time. I went along again to see what else they needed to know but frankly felt a bit uneasy. I had the feeling that they thought I was more style than substance. Being a 23 year old with such a track record of engaging with so many different types of people, I wasn't quite sure how to take it. I wasn't an old Etonian with wealthy parents who had managed to get me a meeting with him because they shared mutual friends. I was from quite humble beginnings and worked extremely hard for the little success that I had managed to acquire.

To make things worse, I had already been through a very tough ordeal to be selected as one of the 25 and was now sitting before this entrepreneur and his strategy coordinator. I explained to them that my CV would show them that I was a grafter and we left the meeting with me firmly remembering just who I was. I emailed him straight after to thank him for the opportunity but then said that I didn't think that I was what he would be looking for. He replied saying 'fair enough' if that was how I felt. I did remain very inspired by what this political entrepreneur had achieved and still hold him in the highest regard. He had managed to combine his passion for business and politics and as a result is someone I look up to a lot. I thought to myself that our stars would once again cross at some point in the future, but until then I needed to carry on working very hard to find a place for me to fit in.

It was very challenging being someone that was still quite young but had managed to have the privilege of experiencing so many different things. It meant that I was quite limited in the things that I could do as I was either over qualified or relatively under experienced in years. I continued to build my business network and managed to carve out a space as a young businessman. I've been able to advise many different organisations across various sectors from small start-ups to large public limited companies. I also began to advise faith groups and set up the Christian Professionals Network in the UK. The aim was to see how faith groups could better engage in the delivery of community services. Some of the success stories included helping to secure a local government contract for one of the largest churches in England. My future in business looked promising as I now wished to add an international aspect to my overall portfolio of experiences. I would later return to Elevation Networks on a part time basis to assist with its international expansion. I also continued to be a part of various going concerns from a strategic advisory position.

Chapter 7

Entering Politics

I am sure that many people will anticipate this chapter to be one of the least exciting of this book. My hope is that as you read this, politics will become just as fascinating to you as it has become to me. In such a short space of time I have experienced political highs and lows, and my firm conviction is that politics is the most powerful institution in the natural world. Politics is the science by which nations are governed, resources are managed, and laws are made. There is no other vehicle in our natural world that allows such power to be both organised and maintained. Some would argue that businesses can be seen to have just as much, if not more, power than those in governments. I would argue that it is government first and foremost that determines how, where, and when, businesses can flourish, if at all. Hopefully my experiences described in this chapter will help to demonstrate why I have arrived at such a conclusion.

As mentioned in previous chapters, I joined the Conservative party in May 5th 2008. I had perfect peace with my decision and knew that this would be the start of a very interesting journey. Shortly after I joined the Conservatives, a meeting was arranged with Pastor Nims and I decided to go with Barbara. This was just after Barbara had also decided to join the Conservative party too, but the meeting was actually about something we were trying to do with Elevation Networks.

During the meeting we discussed a range of things and then I eventually told Pastor Nims that we had decided to join the Conservatives. He said that he believed this was a new trend and that quite a few young people were now thinking about doing this too. He thought it was important to look into the reasons why this was happening. He then picked up his phone to call someone. I never knew who it was at the time, but he put his phone on speakerphone and introduced us to a lady who worked at Conservative Central Office. Elizabeth Berridge, who afterwards became a Conservative Peer, was the Executive Director of the Conservative Christian Fellowship, more commonly known as CCF. David Burrowes, now a Conservative Member of Parliament, and Tim Montgomerie, who went on to found and now edits Conservative Home and Conservative Intelligence, established CCF whilst studying at Exeter University. It had grown to become one of the largest groups within the party. Barbara and I arranged to meet Elizabeth Berridge in Parliament shortly after and had an interesting conversation with her. We told her about who we were and what we did, and she was very helpful in advising us on what we did next from a political prospective. At this point I did get the feeling that she felt Barbara was a bit more advanced than me in regards to our respective careers, as Barbara had already worked for a Member of Parliament... albeit a Labour Member. This inspiring lady would go on to be someone that was instrumental in my political journey for years to come.

After I had graduated from Brunel University, Barbara and I joined CCF's Under 35s development programme. This was a 10 month programme that helped to lay the foundations for Christians interested in politics. You didn't have to be a Conservative to be a part of the programme, it was designed to help you to understand what it was you believed in as a Christian interested in politics. The programme had so many different speakers, ranging from Members of Parliament, Members of the House of Lords, policy makers, people from think tanks, non party political church ministers, and other key Christians who had experience and insight into the many levels of functioning as a Christian in the world of politics.

I learnt so much, and was challenged regularly by these great people who were coming to speak to us. I doubt very much that there is any course like it anywhere in Britain, and it was a privilege to have been selected to be involved in such a thing. Part of the programme also required you to have a mentor from the world of politics and I was fortunate to meet a then Shadow Minister who went on to mentor me for over two years. He was a Shadow Minister at the Department for Work & Pensions, so we shared similar interests in regards to unemployment in the UK.

I combined my time on the course with my Masters degree in Ethnicity, Migration, and Policy. Studying a Masters was another way of ensuring I was increasing my skills whilst also continuing to pursue business and political interests. The classes were full of very left leaning individuals who were very well read. They would discuss things that were way over my head initially because I had not studied this social science before. My undergraduate degree was of course in Business & Management Accounting which had very little policy content besides an economics module.

To make things more interesting, at the same time I was referred to an educational psychologist who diagnosed me with dyslexia and dyspraxia. At first I thought it wouldn't affect me, but as I left the office of the psychologist I found myself feeling sombre. I began to reflect on my previous years of studying and couldn't help but wonder if I would have achieved more if I had known earlier. Would I have managed to get the 1st class degree that all university students strive for? Were my learning difficulties why I struggled with my behaviour growing up or was this just a psychologist that helped to give people excuses? A lot of things suddenly began to make sense. At the same time I wasn't sure if I wanted to accept the idea of having learning difficulties. It was all a strange experience, but I soon made the decision not to let it change me. Maybe I was being a bit stubborn and should have used this new information to be more conscious of my weaknesses. Either way, it certainly made me more conscious of the fact that I needed to be more aware of my spelling and grammar. It is something that I still struggle with today.

I was in a very interesting place where on one hand I was engaging with some of the most excellent conservative thinkers who held the highest offices in the land, and on the other I was in classes with very intelligent left wing academics. It all made for a very interesting learning experience and it really helped to shape my own political ideas today. Whilst I may be a Conservative, I certainly sympathise with the challenges that occur through the lack of representation of many groups within power structures. I also appreciate the role that social class continues to play in society as a whole. In addition I believe that although most people may not want this to be the case, race is still a social construct that marginalises many groups within communities across the world today.

Even within nations where most people have similar skin tones, there are still tribal biases that show us that human nature likes to create an 'other'. Since the beginning of time, people have justified their own existence through the creation of identities that allow them to differentiate themselves from other people. Of course if the world ever decided to realise that in reality there is just one race, the human race, nothing would be impossible for us to do. We'd literally be able to make the world whatever it is that we would want it to be. But for now less people hold power and more people in our world continue to suffer. At the same time I believe like Ghandi that we as individuals 'must be the change that we wish to see in the world'. We cannot simply rely on governments for every answer as they simply don't have it. Politicians win elections by promising the world but the reality is that they can only ever do so much. They have limited resources which mean that if they spend more in one place then money must be redistributed from another. It also means that if they come up with a new idea then an old policy must be dropped. I learnt this lesson very well in my business when the change of government in 2010 meant that we missed out on the opportunity to secure large contracts and quickly had to adapt to new policies.

So the foundations of my own personal political beliefs

and ideas began to take shape as I was engaging with both left and right wing ideas. I became more confident on what it was that I represented, however I was conscious not to be explicitly Conservative at times. It wasn't something that I dared to speak up about boldly during my Masters lectures; however I did mention it to my personal tutor who was quite perplexed about the political choice that I had made.

People eventually began to recognise me as a Conservative and I'd start many debates where I discussed my political disposition. I would meet my parliamentary mentor, the Shadow Minister, every so often too, and he'd listen to what I was up to and would give me some advice on what he felt was the best thing for me to do next.

I was balancing all of this with the work I was doing back then with Elevation Networks, which was still my priority at this point. In one of our meetings towards the end of 2009, my mentor suggested that I get involved with my local council. For some reason I had a perception of a local council being full of very old people and the whole thing being rather boring. I'm not sure where I had this perception from but because of it I wasn't very keen to get involved in local government, but I took his advice anyway. I sent my local MP an email where I told her who I was and what I did. She forwarded the message onto one of my local Councillors. He also worked for London Mayor and the Conservative members of the Greater London Authority (GLA) and invited me to meet him at London Bridge. He was such a nice guy and we had a very rich conversation.

Towards the end of the meeting he said to me, "So are you interested?" I wasn't too sure what he was talking about, but he then made it clear that he thought I would make a great local councillor. I was a bit taken aback as I'd never really thought about the prospect of being so involved in local government. I don't think my local government ambitions ever really went past helping to distribute leaflets. I said I wasn't sure that I'd be interested in such a role, but then he began to sell the vision and I left the meeting reflecting on whether I could ever do such a thing.

By this time all of the candidates for the May 2010 local council elections had already been selected and I thought it would probably be a while before I had to think about this again. To my surprise a Councillor in the ward (area) next to where I lived decided that she wanted to step down from her position. This meant that there would potentially be a candidacy up for grabs if I was interested in taking it. I went to visit the then head of the council and I think she liked me. I wasn't quite sure what to make of her as she was a very direct lady and she reminded me very much of Margaret Thatcher. They put my name forward to the ward chairman and one of the other Conservative councillors where the council seat had become available and we arranged to meet up close to the area. I went along to see them not knowing what to expect. To my surprise there was a good cop and a bad cop. The good cop (ward chairman) was very welcoming but the bad cop (councillor) was quite arrogant and negative about the whole idea of me running. What I didn't know at the time was that they ultimately would decide who was selected as the candidate because they would be influencing the rest of the voters. I was about to experience a type of politics that I had not experienced before.

After we finished the meeting I wasn't too sure what to make of the whole situation. Was I really going to put myself forward to work side by side with this highly arrogant individual who I was sure never even lived in the borough? Eventually I decided to apply anyway and filled out the relevant forms. I was invited for a first interview with the chairmen from the constituency wards. The room was arranged in a semi circle, with me facing all of the chairmen. It was all quite intimidating at first but I made sure I performed to the best of my abilities.

I got through to the next round in which the ward association members would be voting for their respective candidate. I arrived at the second round interview directly from a meeting in Leicester and so was very unsettled by the time I eventually reached the venue in Barnet. I tried to settle down as best I could before I went in for the interview. The audience was now a lot smaller than before but I wasn't very settled. I spoke quite fast and there was a lady at the front that struggled to hear what I was saying. I stuck to my areas of strength to answer many of the questions, and was very strong when discussing issues such as youth unemployment and engaging new members to the association. I knew that I could have done a lot better, but I also knew that it was likely that I had done very well compared to others who had gone for the seat.

My competition included a funeral director, and I was certain that his profession would not be a vote winner by any stretch of the imagination. Once the interviews had finished there was a secret ballot and votes were counted in front of us. I ended up finishing second to a gentleman who I was told had more campaigning experience than me. I was pulled to the side by someone who told me that I was a very strong candidate and that I shouldn't be upset by my performance. She told me that if I had come a few months back when all of the seats in the borough were up for grabs, I would have certainly been selected as a candidate for a seat in the borough. I took great heart from the fact that I was viewed as a quality candidate, but I also had the feeling that the whole process wasn't as black and white as maybe I antici- pated it would be. This didn't seem to be a fair fight and I had a problem with that. It later emerged that my name was indeed put forward by the head of the council to go for the council seat. However certain people who were voting that evening may not have favoured a candidate who had been put forward by the council leader for personal and political reasons. It also emerged that the ward chairman had called up a Member of Parliament who knew me because he thought that my story was 'too good to be true'. The chairman also advised the people voting that night on which candidate they should pick, which was of course the candi- date that eventually was selected.

All of this completely offended me and I was not sure if I could bear engaging with a system that seemed unfair and a bit dodgy. This was my moment of disillusionment with politics, the time that most people have in their lives when they believe that politics is a corrupted science full of people that aren't to be trusted. Most people decide to do one of two things after they experience such a crisis; they either choose to disengage from the whole process or they choose to become some form of external entity that is designed to put pressure on those within the political system. It never took me too long to decide what it was I was going to do. I chose to take the road less travelled. I decided that I wasn't going to take this situation lightly and I was going to come back stronger from it. I was going to rise above the situation, forgive the people that had clearly blocked my path, and not get bitter but get better. I was going to show people that those with the right motives and agendas can win the political game and would be able to bring about the change that they wish to see. I wasn't sure how, when, or where, but one day I would be able to be an example and people would do more than I did because of the example that I was.

I began to campaign for the local councillors in my ward, and also started to attend local association events in order for people to begin to know who I was. As much as I wasn't happy with the whole selection process which I had just been through, I recognised that there was a lack of relationship between me and the people that were selecting the candidates and as a result they had no real reason to trust that I would do well for them. I needed to be a trusted part of the political community before I could justify holding any position of influence. I carried on campaigning for Parliamentary Candidates across London, including the then Shadow Transport Secretary Theresa Villiars MP, David Burrowes MP, and the former chief executive of the Centre for Social Justice; Philippa Stroud. I was attending events in Parliament too, and was still on the Conservative Christian Fellowship's under 35s course. I was getting more involved in politics, but this was still early days. I met up with the chairman of the ward where I was unsuccessfully selected, and he was very honest about the whole situation, which I guess was honourable. He did say that he believed my time to shine would eventually come, but not just yet. I wasn't sure if I ever wanted to run for a council seat again, but I was happy to be involved and thought that it wasn't something I would need to think about until probably much closer to the next elections at the earliest.

The 2010 Local and General Elections were the first elections that I had been directly involved in and it was therefore a very special moment for me. To see the manpower that goes into campaigning in the build up to the big day, and also the activities on the day itself, was all very insightful. I volunteered as a teller on Election Day; the activists that wait outside of respective polling stations to collect your voter registration number after you've voted. This would allow us to know which of our supporters had been out to vote. I would then report back to the central meeting point and those who were Conservative supporters that had not voted yet would be politely encouraged to come out before the polling stations were closed. I was tired by the end of the Election Day but tried to stay up to see as many of the results as possible. Of course by the time I had woken up no single party had won the election with a clear majority so things were not as straight forward as most people would have wanted. I was more concerned to see whether or not my local councillors had won.

Thankfully all the councillors that I campaigned for in my ward were duly elected. The arrogant councillor that I had met in the ward next door surprisingly lost his seat and disappeared very quickly afterwards. I was later told that he had said some very upsetting things about his own constituents and it had been published in the local newspaper. It was sad to see anyone lose their seat and it wasn't something I wanted to take any joy in seeing, even if he was a bit arrogant. I waited like most of the British public to see what the outcome of this hung parliament would be.

When the coalition agreement was eventually settled I watched our new Prime Minister, David Cameron, give his speech outside Downing Street with the opening words "Her Majesty the Queen has asked me to form a government." It was a moment that I don't think I'll ever forget. All of this man's hard work had now taken him to the pinnacle of his political career and he was now the Prime Minister. I was witnessing his moment in history, and it made me more inspired to have my own one day.

With the experiences of the 2010 Local and General Elections behind me, I tried to focus as much as I could on my immediate challenge, which as the previous chapter showed was making Elevation Networks a sustainable organisation. I had been out of university for a year by this time, and things weren't the best financially. I was making some money through delivering various training for organisations like the National Youth Agency, and was also beginning to get to grips with my Masters degree. But I still wasn't quite established enough both to sustain myself financially and to support my Mother at home.

This was also the time that I began to understand the role of local government. I started to read the politics section on the BBC News website a lot more than the business section, and became hooked on the leading website for Conservatives; Conservative Home, just like many other Conservative activists. This was the time when my head was turning towards politics and my family started to notice it. For my Mum, the idea of her son becoming a politician one day was an answer to a daily prayer, but at the same time it also meant that I was chasing another dream as opposed to settling down with a stable job. This constant struggle between being very proud of my achievements and wanting me to bring home some money would play out for a long time with my Mother and me. It must of course be said that most people involved in politics have sacrificed the opportunity for paid work for significant periods of time in order to gain the much needed experience to break into this very competitive environment. Of course many of the people that have reached the pinnacle of politics have also been from quite well off backgrounds and could probably afford not to work and not to be contributing to household bills.

At this point I still believed that politics would be where I would end up in the long term, but for now I needed to find out how to continue making a difference in the short to medium term. I thought that I had found exactly what could potentially fill this void when I heard some very interesting news towards the end of 2010. Elizabeth Berridge, the director of CCF who had helped me so much in my political journey, was offered a peerage by the new Prime Minister David Cameron. Elizabeth Berridge would now be Baroness Berridge, a Member of the House of Lords, and as a result they would be looking for a new director of the CCF to replace her. This was my opportunity to take on a role that was perfectly aligned to my passions and experiences. CCF did events, had members, and promoted a social agenda, everything that Elevation Networks was doing but with a different cause. I had been on their development course, went to one of the largest churches that CCF was aligned with, and was of course Christian. I created a strong strategic plan to grow the organisation and handed in a very strong application, backed by very influential people. Unfortunately I was once again unsuccessful with my bid to break into politics as I wasn't selected to be interviewed by CCF. Initially it made me very disappointed, but then it motivated me even more to push on. Politics was where I belonged, and these setbacks made me realise this very fact. For indeed if I was unable to break into such a system, even with my experience and current networks, then what hope would most of the other people that were not part of these networks have of breaking into politics? This was a big issue for me, and something I needed to help to fix. Politics was where I belonged, and I needed to make sure I did everything that I could to become the leader I believed I could be. There was no real plan, but I knew I was going to hopefully have enough connections to influence policy one day. Not too long after this was the moment that was written about in the previous chapter; when I decided it was time for me to focus more on politics and step down from the day to day running of Elevation Networks.

In October 2011 I attended my first Conservative Party

Conference. I went with staff members from the Greater London Authority (GLA) but really used this as my own fact finding mission. The first thing I noticed was that there were very few people from ethnic minorities at the conference. The ones that were there were almost apologetic and very consciously seemed to avoid eye contact with other people of the same ethnicity. That there were so many events targeted at different political areas made it difficult to pick just where to go. Conference was a place that was full of ideas, where you could meet the key policy makers. I remember going to my first event at conference and being able ask Oliver Letwin MP two questions. He is a current Minister in the Cabinet Office, and oversees the Party's policy implementation strategy. I asked him about youth unemployment and the possible closure of the Youth Justice Board for England & Wales. It was very clear that the media and politicians had a very cosy relationship too. I would be amazed to see well known journalists in the bar with policy makers having a drink and sharing jokes like old friends. This was of course very different to the perceptions of independent media coverage that everyone would hope the general public would believe was the case. You could argue that it is very difficult not to build a relationship with people that you are paid to follow around, and in some respects that very relationship is what allows you to get stories that would otherwise never be known to the public. Nonetheless it was something that perplexed me during my first conference. It really helped that I knew members of the GLA, and some other key people that encouraged me on my political journey. They would introduce me to their friends quite freely, and it all gave me an opportunity to network and establish new links. This was the first time that I had an opportunity to be myself within a new political environment, as opposed to Samuel who was a member of the Conservative Christian Fellowship or Samuel who was a young black Conservative in East Barnet ward. CCF was all that I really knew in regards to Conservative political groups, so conference opened up my eyes to the many other organisations in and around the party. I came across interesting groups like the Bow Group, through which I would later launch my first policy paper.

I wanted to make sure that I spent my time at conference wisely and so I chose to go to events that catered for my areas of passion. Of the hundreds of events and meetings being put on, I realised that there was only one event on winning votes from communities that usually don't vote for Conservative, notably ethnic minority communities. This was certainly an area of interest to me so I went along. The fringe event was put on by two leading think tanks, Demos and the Runnymede Trust. I noticed that the director of Runnymede looked a bit uncomfortable being there, and very quickly realised that he obviously wasn't a fan of Conservatives. I later found out that the director of Demos was actually quite a controversial figure himself. I found it quite strange that a liberal think tank and a think tank founded on Labour principles were the only ones to put on an event of this nature.

I was also invited to the launch of a new group called Conservative Friends of International Development (CFID). This event sounded very interesting to me, so I made sure I went along. To my surprise, by the time I had gone to the room where this event was being held, it was completely full. I decided to wait patiently outside to see if I could hear the Secretary of State for International Development, Andrew Mitchell MP, speak. Once he had finished, one of his assistance spotted me and grabbed me. She took me straight to meet Andrew Mitchell. She said she was impressed that I waited outside patiently and this is why she wanted to make the introduction. I was a bit stunned so had very little to say but it was very good to meet him. She then introduced me to his Parliamentary Private Secretary (PPS). A PPS is a Member of Parliament that bridges the gap between other Members of Parliament and Ministers in government. They help to relay any policy matters that backbenchers could be having and also help to ensure parliament progresses with few rebellions- well at least that's the theory of the role of PPS.

Being introduced to the Secretary of State taught me a

very valuable lesson. I learnt that being patient and humble really does work. I could have been aggressive and tried to force my way in, but then I'd have been just another number in the crowd. Instead I waited patiently and I got more than I bargained for. CFID would in the months ahead give me some very amazing experiences, including the privilege of sitting very close to Bill Gates when he came to speak to CFID members in parliament in November 2011. It was all very surreal, and until it actually happened I wasn't convinced that the event was actually going to happen.

Hearing Bill Gates speak about the role he's playing in developing nations was very inspiring. The biggest revelation of his speech for me however was the role government plays in society. It was settled in my heart that government was the most powerful structure in the natural world. I concluded this after seeing how one of the richest men of my generation was making the case to government to continue to do more in an area he was evidently passionate about. If Bill Gates himself could not do all he desired without the involvement of government, then it was clear to me that governments across the world, big or small, maintain and coordinate power more than any wealthy individual. This further motivated me to see how I could make a difference within government and politics. Thankfully, from this point on things started to finally click for me in the world of politics.

The end of 2011 saw me oversee the second year of the Elevation Networks nationwide debate tour. This was now the largest forum of its kind in the UK, and targeted black & Asian students in an attempt to get them more involved in public life. 'The Great Debate Tour' wasn't only an opportunity for us to engage ethnic minority students in the UK with politics, but was also an opportunity for me personally to listen and learn from the experiences of what many of the different students had been through. What was very strange was the variety of perspectives amongst what many people classify as one homogeneous group. We had to ensure that the debate was accessible to everyone who attended, and were conscious that different universities had students who were at different levels of engagement. This wasn't just about where universities were in league tables, but also where they were geographically, and what sort of subjects the students on the campuses were likely to study, and what kind of individuals each debate would be likely to attract.

For example, we knew that students at Cambridge would be very different to those at Oxford, as we ran Cambridge debates through their left wing Black Students Campaign, whereas we ran Oxford's debates through their African & Caribbean Society, which had a lot more political diversity. When we visited Oxford, I could see that although many in the room were articulate and very learned, they also had very different experiences growing up. Some had come from inner city areas, and had managed to overcome barriers due to support from parents and local programmes for young people who showed great potential. As a result, these students were very aware of the challenges some of their peers that they had left behind were still facing in regards to unemployment and social deprivation. I found these students very interesting, and felt that their experiences could be very valuable to the next generation. On the other hand there were other black students that were evidently from quite sheltered backgrounds. They could not relate at all to the adverse statistics and negative media coverage of black people. They were from areas where black people were very much in the minority and as a result they weren't really that passionate about any desire for a sense of 'community action' or helping to fix any social challenges linked to this group. For those students, being black had little to no meaning, and wasn't something they were too keen to hang onto as they progressed into the inevitable success that comes from studying at such institutions. They thought that if they could end up at Oxford, then of course no one else really had an excuse for not self-actualising. I sort of felt sorry for these evidently ignorant individuals who would really have no reason ever to have an epiphany. The reality is that life was, and still is, not that straight forward. Where you live, where you study, the social class you are born into, and your ethnic background, still all come together to form a profile of where you are likely to end up in life. In an ideal world of course this wouldn't be the case, but ideals are the very reason why we must all engage with politics! There is no benefit to society for being ignorant of inequalities. We must first acknowledge they do exist and then find ways to eradicate them.

I once wrote an article for the Tory Reform Group's Social Mobility Pamphlet, which is in the final section of this book, where I spoke about the desire for all three major parties to be seen as champions of social mobility. I wrote that although it's something many want to be associated with, the reality is that we have a current economic situation that limits their ability to engage proactively with the idea of perfect social mobility. It is less of a priority than most would like us to think.

On deeper reflection, Oxford was, and probably still is, a fair reflection of the current black members of the political classes. We have one or two that feel they have a moral obligation to be a voice for the communities they came from or represent. The likes of Dianne Abbott MP from Labour and Shaun Bailey of the Conservatives seem to unapologetically speak out for their communities, sometimes in ways that can only be described as controversial. The majority, particularly the Conservative black politicians, do at times give me the feeling that this collective experience that many people speak of is simply not what they can relate to. They studied at Oxford, they are from privileged backgrounds, and they do not share the same experiences as the majority of the people from the same ethnic background. This of course is one of the greatest challenges that the Conservative party faces. At this present time 1 in 4 pupils in UK primary schools are from an ethnic minority background. According to the Runnymede Trust, by 2051, 1 in 5 UK citizens will be from an ethnic minority.

Unfortunately current figures don't lie when looking at the experiences of many ethnic minority communities. 75% of African & Caribbean's in the UK live in 88 of the poorest wards in the country. Bangladeshi students are amongst the worst academic performers in the land, and of course we know that ethnic minority communities are overall over-represented within the criminal justice system. This has meant that in many respects, poverty and race has become at times interlinked, and the debate has emerged as to whether there is any longer a thing as race discrimination, or if all inequalities are simply down to class.

My response would be that politics is as much about perception as it is about reality. We can debate till the cows come home as to whether or not race discrimination still exists, but the reality is that communities still feel this is very much a problem and as a result policies must account for this. The Conservative party at the moment must find a way to attract future leaders who have true conservative values, but at the same time have the desire to reach out to communities that need to be won over if we are ever to command a strong majority in tomorrow's changing world. This of course doesn't just extend to ethnic minority communities, but also to people from working class backgrounds, and those in the Northern parts of the United Kingdom.

For this to happen there must be a sense of One Nation Conservatism that demonstrates a vision for the country which everyone can identify with and buy into. The party simply must be seen to be a party for all. This is a challenge that I feel the party must rise to, and I hope to play a significant role in helping to make this happen.

In light of the above, I joined the Tory Reform Group (TRG) in early 2012. It seemed like the natural place to belong politically as its values to a large extent are similar to my own. The group was formed in 1975 as an independent, but party aligned, organisation for Conservative members. The underpinning philosophy of TRG is around finding ways to create economic efficiency, whilst not losing the necessary compassion to ensure that the most vulnerable in society are cared for. TRG was where I felt I could be around conservatives who had similar ideas of how the country could be run effectively, and to my delight I was embraced with open arms.

I was invited to come along to their AGM, and to their annual dinner, where former Deputy Prime Minister, Lord Heseltine was to be the key note speaker. What I did not know at the time was that the Member of Parliament hosting the event was to be the same Member that I had arranged to meet the day before. I had first met him at an All Party Parliamentary Group (APPG) meeting on race relations a few months before. The particular person was, and still is, one of the most interesting politicians I'd ever met. He is very down to earth, and his journey into Parliament included him working around the world for many years. This resulted in him having a slight accent that I noticed early on. At the TRG dinner, I was put on Table 1 with Lord Heseltine and my new MP friend. I sat next to Mrs Heseltine, who introduced me to her husband at the end of the night. She told him I was keen to get more involved in politics, to which he replied in his famously direct style, "I have helped many people like you to get elected into Parliament. It is very difficult, but you must never give up". Of course he was referring to my colour, but I will never forget those few words. I think a former Deputy Prime Minister saying that you are never to give up is something worth remembering. Of course he had nothing to lose as he had been to the pinnacle of politics and business, and so his direct way of communicating was much to be respected.

I certainly had no divine right to be at the top table for this event, and the rest of the room were probably wondering why it was that I was there. Even more surprisingly, during his speech, the politician that I had only met properly the day before decided to praise my contributions to the Party. He very quickly became arguably my main politically ally and would continue to look out for me as I navigated through the political minefield. He is one the many supporters one needs when trying to progress in life. He was very honest with me and told me what he thought I should be doing going forward in politics. As a Patron of the Tory Reform Group, our political ideas were quite similar in some respects, and we shared the same policy interests, namely business, enterprise, youth and equality. This was probably partly why I was successfully voted onto the management board of the Tory Reform Group shortly after the event.

When he asked me to come to work for him in Parliament, I didn't need to think too much before accepting. This parliamentarian was one of the first people in politics who I really felt cared about me succeeding. He believed I had the potential to add value to the party, and was happy for me to combine my business activities with working for him a few days a week in Parliament.

I would work on special projects that would demonstrate to the Party what I could do, and would also allow me to learn more about how Parliament works. It felt like finally, after just over a year of working hard to break into politics, I was now succeeding. My political network was growing, I was now actively working in Parliament on projects that were closely aligned with my passions and experiences, and most importantly; I was still given the flexibility to pursue what I felt was unfinished business in the world of social entrepreneurship. I was well and truly on the road to WINNING THE RACE. I began to write more and more about my ideas, and became a lot more confident about why I had chosen to take this particular political path. I was now ready to debate with anyone about what it was that I believed and why I felt that the centre right still had the potential to have an equality agenda that was relevant to all. The challenge was of course that I also ran the risk of being seen as a single issue political thinker. Equality was not the most popular theme to pick up as a Conservative, but I truly believed that in the years to come; taking up this battle would prove to have been the right thing to do on many levels.

There have been other highs and lows on my political journey to date which have allowed me to develop the thick skin needed to engage in such an environment. Certainly a highlight was meeting the Prime Minister, David Cameron, for the first time. He was much taller than I imagined, and we had a good conversation about the government's Work Programme. Of course Mr Cameron probably wouldn't remember our conversation, but the picture of this conversation was captured and used. I met Mr Cameron at a special reception for nominees for the Spirit of London Awards in Downing Street. I remember leaving the reception a little early as I usually would do on such occasions, and just as I was trying to locate the exit the Prime Minister was also leaving, and for around 5 seconds we were both walking down a set of stairs alone, with his aides waiting for him at the bottom of the stairs. Mr Cameron then went through a door which I can only assume led to his offices or his flat. I remember thinking 'gosh that was 'awkward'. I didn't really know what to do in those short five or so seconds. I mean, it's not very often that one is in Downing Street, let alone in a place where it's just you and the Prime Minister. I figured that it was probably best that I left him alone as he was likely to have had a long day and besides stopping a Prime Minister on his way somewhere in Downing Street could have ended very badly for me. I wasn't quite ready to be thrown out by armed guards in front of the general public. I did get the strange feeling that one day I'd be back, and that one day I'd find out what was behind those doors.

I've also had the privilege of going to the Speaker's House in Parliament for a reception for the Christian's in Parliament group. The Speaker's House is probably the most beautiful part of the Palace of Westminster. The preacher, Rob Parsons, spoke very articulately at the event about what it means to love, and the challenges of fighting for what is right in politics. Other highlights included the first time I had an article published on Conservative Home. I wasn't sure when it would be up, but one Wednesday morning I logged onto the website and there it was. I felt very proud that one of my pieces was up and I didn't take the comments of some of the more right wing readers too seriously. The article did result in me being able to get some of my friends a bit more involved and aware of Conservative politics which was good, and till this day a lot of people I meet in politics have read the piece.

Having my first research report published by the oldest

centre right think tank in Britain, the Bow Group, was another significant moment in my political walk. I had managed to take the conversation of race equality to a new audience, which was part of my personal mission. We managed to launch the report in one of the largest rooms in Parliament; the same room where I had seen Bill Gates speak so eloquently in November 2011. All of this motivated me to want to do more in politics, and hopefully to make more of a difference to the communities that at times have had little to no voice in the current political system. I continued to attend All Party Parliamentary Group meetings around topics that focused on areas of particular interest to me, and have written a number articles that I hope were thought provoking for various media outlets. I am also the first ever columnist for Nigerian Watch, a UK based newspaper with an estimated readership of 500,000.

There was a point when I was going to end up working full time at the Greater London Authority (GLA). The Conservatives had a role around the 2012 Olympic legacy. This time, I was the one with the advantage. I was good friends with the head of staff who was keen for me to apply. I would have probably ended up working there had it not been for another role that came up at Conservative Campaign Headquarters (CCHQ). They were looking for a race and faith advisor, two areas very close to me of course. I applied, but there was a lot of delay in them getting back to anyone about the role at CCHQ, and I took the risk of turning down the role at the GLA in the hope that I would have a chance of getting the advisor role. Once again to my surprise I did not get the role. I was told later that no one in fact got the position. I guess if I had been successful in getting the role I would have never been able to have had the flexibility of balancing it with a life in business, and so things certainly have worked out quite well. I would reckon that the people that have been successful in politics, and probably in most other areas of life, have had to deal with many setbacks. One must be quick to recover and to keep on going, and eventually success will come to those who are persistent.

I'm really enjoying being in Parliament every week and engaging with such great and influential minds. My current work sees me navigating my way across Whitehall, sometimes even having the privilege of attending meetings at Number 10. I still get a little lost sometimes within the Palace of Westminster, but I am sure in time it'll all be very natural to me. Some of my work includes helping to launch a leadership programme for the Conservative Party, identifying top talent from communities that do not traditionally vote Conservative and exposing them to the very highest power structures in the land. I am also assisting in helping Members of Parliament across all the three major parties in establishing a business fund to invest in their constituencies. It's a great initiative that was birthed by Richard Fuller, Member for Bedford.

Of course my main objective is to be actively helping to make politics more accessible for people who are like me. I want one day to ensure that I have helped to open up politics to people from working class backgrounds, ethnic minorities, and those who have aspirations to help make the country a greater place for everyone. I am only one man, and so I'll need a lot of grace, a lot of good people with the same vision, and the resources to make such a dream a reality. But I've seen enough of all the above to be very hopeful indeed!

Chapter 8

Relationships

This chapter is probably the one that will mean the most of all to readers and to me. It is the one that focuses on the most precious thing that any of us have – relationships. All of our lives are full of moments when relationships have been what have defined anything good or bad that has happened to us, and for myself my time after leaving Brunel University has been shaped by the quality of my own relationships.

In the previous chapters I discussed how my failure to maintain a relationship with my most trusted deputy had resulted in me initially losing a friend. The good news is that today we once again have a great relationship and are still on very similar journeys, but of course in our own ways. Whilst Jamal has been doing amazing work helping young fathers in London and extending his own enterprise to West Africa, I have been focusing on business and politics, mainly in the UK. We both became engaged in 2011 to two very beautiful women and I am sure that our friendship will last for many years to come. There are also many other relationships that have helped to shape who I am today and I hope that I can give as many of them as much credit as they deserve in this chapter.

I'll begin with my relationship with the many mentors that I have today. My first ever mentor was a gentleman that for the sake of this book I will call Mr OJ. He is a consultant for an IT system called SAP. He used to work for PriceWaterhouse and is an expert in business strategy. I met him when I was volunteering for the bookshop in my church and decided to ask him to be my mentor. What made me approach him was the fact that he had written a book which was actually on sale in the bookshop at the time. I was really impressed by the fact that he'd manage to write a whole book and was also flying across the world consulting for people. Over the past few years he has been arguably one of the most valuable people in my life. He has taught me many of the tools that I use to support the young people who I mentor, and continues to help me to give my thoughts a definite shape. I couldn't have achieved many of the things that I have done if it wasn't for Mr OJ's sound wisdom and I will forever be grateful for how he has always been there to advise me when I have needed his words of wisdom.

Every year I sit down with Mr OJ to talk through my plans for the year ahead, and he critiques the things that I have written. That really helps me to think about how I will imple- ment the plans practically. I cannot praise him and thank him enough for all of his support, and it has shown me just how important it is to have a mentor in your life.

I'm fortunate to have many other people that contribute to my life regularly. Another mentor of mine is the deputy pastor of my church. He oversees the operations of what is one of the largest churches in the UK, and also oversees the largest bi-annual Christian gathering in Europe, the Festival of Life. In addition to this, he is a qualified medical doctor (but no longer practises) and also has an MBA. Although I do not see him too often because we can both be quite busy, when- ever there is an emergency situation or a crisis he is the one that I go to for advice that will help to realign my thoughts. He has never failed to deliver, and was in fact the mentor that I went to visit when I did not know how to deal with the situ- ation with Jamal. It was his advice that ensured I made sure I operated with the upmost integrity, and it also allowed me to see things from Jamal's prospective.

Other close advisors of mine include Sir Terry Mansfield CBE. He is the former President of the National Magazine Company, owners of Reveal, Cosmopolitan, Red Magazine and many others. We both sit on the Peace Alliance board together. Sir Terry is very well connected and very honest in his perspective of what I should be doing to grow as a young man attempting to become very influential. I'm very grateful for his support, particularly when he arranged for me to visit the headquarters of the Big Issue publication.

It was very inspiring to meet their Chief Executive and to see the great work that they do. I'm also fortunate to have a number of Members of Parliament who are happy to give me advice and guidance. A few MPs in particular have been pivotal in helping me progress in politics. The list of supporters and mentors who have advised me over the years is very long and could go on for many pages. They include the Head of Office for the Conservatives at the Greater London Authority (GLA), the Chief Executive of a FTSE 250 company with a turnover of over £2 billion, the former Executive Director of the Conservative Christian Fellowship, the Chief Executive of the Peace Alliance, all of my pastors at my local church, and Jennifer who was the Head of Diversity at the investment bank that supported Elevation Networks first. She was the first corporate to give us a chance, and always believed in us and so much of my success is as a result of her support. These are just some of the people who have been there to instruct and guide me.

I've also had a tight inner circle of friends over the years that have enriched my life on this journey so far. The value of an inner circle to anyone in any walk of life cannot be underestimated. My personal life mission is very clear. The only thing that may be blurry at times is how this will manifest itself through various roles and activities. But over the years there have been some people that have decided to join me on this journey.

One of these people is a young man who I met whilst visiting another church. I noticed that he was a very humble individual and decided to offer him a spare ticket that I had to a Chelsea FA Cup game. I love the idea of being able to provide opportunities for people and a ticket to see a Premier League club is a dream come true for many young people across the country. This person was 17 years old when I met him and he wanted to become a sports journalist at the time. Fast forward years later and today he is the President of Goldsmiths' Students' Union. He has also been the Vice President of his union, as well as the Vice-President of his African & Caribbean Society, and is also a member of Elevation Networks' wider strategy team. He is someone that has been a loyal servant and I have always been able to rely on him. He is someone that I can trust and is one of those people who buy into me first and then my vision. Come rain or shine he is loyal and as a result is more like a friend than a mentee.

The same can be said for another young man that I met in 2008. Francis really wanted a meeting with me, and when I sat with him eventually that December I had no idea that he would actually implement more or less everything that I advised him to do. He managed to set up a society, start up his own enterprise, and eventually became the President of his student union at London Southbank University. This young man is a leader within his own right and has been someone that I have seen grow over the years. He has inspired so many people who have lost hope for one reason or another and represents what it really means to be a community leader. His politics is a bit different from my own but I still count him as a member of my inner circle and I'm very proud to be a part of his own personal journey.

I can say the same about quite a few of the young people that I mentor and feel that they are very valuable people to me. These young men are from very non traditional backgrounds and I trust that in the years to come they will be leading figures in their chosen occupations. Not all of them have chosen to take similar paths to me, like my good friend Dennis. He chose not to follow the path of his brother, who was the first black President of Cambridge Students' Union, and instead chose to go straight into employment. He's now a director of a firm at the age of 21, and is in the top 10% of earners in the UK. It just goes to show that university is maybe not for everyone.

The strange thing is that although I have advised all these people on how they can carry on growing in their lives, I feel like I can trust them to be there for me more than most people I know. Maybe this type of loyalty is inevitable when someone is there for you but of course this wasn't the motive for me agreeing to be someone who advises them. I guess if I could be there for any of the people that mentor me in any way possible, I would count it a great privilege, and this could be the same feeling that they have for me. There is something special about knowing that someone has your best interest at heart and is giving you tools to become a better person.

There are other friends of mine who have lasted the distance even with us all becoming increasingly busy since university. John, who was the first person that I met at university, went on to be my best man for my wedding and has been ever present in my life since the first day we met. He never became involved in student politics when I did which really helped me from a personal prospective. It was very valuable having friends who were not directly involved with my work, and he has regularly tried to get me not to think about work at times over the years when I was too consumed with what I was doing.

This is the same with Shaun, our housemate in our second year at university. He has also doubled up as one of my personal stylists, and I've taken him clothes shopping with me many times because I really don't like shopping but he seems to love it. I love my whole Brunel University family and am very grateful for what were some of the most fantastic years of my life. I definitely have to thank all of the thousand people who helped to get me elected to the Students' Union back then and everyone else on this journey that I may have forgotten. I certainly never regret my decision to pick Brunel in 2005 and doubt I would have had the same experience anywhere else.

There are also people from my local area in Barnet that I've known since my school days who I value very much. It is very calming at times when I can leave the cares of this world on a Friday night to visit the boys in Barnet where I am still just the boy from around the corner. My friends from church are also people who I value so much because we've seen each other grow on our individual journeys and are part of a larger community which is something that is very rare in this day and age. To know that there are people who care for you and are praying for you is so encouraging, and attending church on a Sunday is both a spiritual, relational, and a social experience in so many ways.

Unfortunately there have also been failed relationships over the years where things never worked out for various reasons. Like many young men commitment to women was a challenge at times as I never really knew what I wanted. There were times when I would get to know a girl and eventually would decide that she wasn't the one for me.

There were quite a few occasions when a female would be very emotionally attached to me by the time I had actually made the decision not to pursue a relationship with her. Most of these were never official relationships and so the damage was arguably limited. By the time I had graduated from university there was less opportunity for these scenarios to happen. However I did start a relationship with a young lady shortly after leaving Brunel. She was a humble and kind person who had the gift of being able to give me the exact piece of advice that I needed at any given time. If I ever needed someone to give me a word of encouragement or to tell me what I was doing was wrong, she was somehow able to say things in the exact way that would ensure I took the advice well.

A writer once referred this type of effective communication as 'a timely word'. The writer said it was like 'apples of gold in pictures of silver'. I have no idea how she learnt that skill but it was something that I valued very much and even relied on to an extent. Our relationship was OK but there was a feeling that we were from two different cultures. I had a very traditionalist (some might say conservative) way of looking at how our relationship needed to be, whereas she was a bit more liberal in her outlook on things. This cultural difference was something that used to affect us and they'd be times when I would start arguments because I did not like the way things were.

Eventually we split up and I knew straight away that the mistake that I had made was not appreciating the fact that you should never try to change someone you are with. Relationships are about two people coming together because they love who the other is. Although both people may not be perfect, the only way that any union will continue for the long term is if both accept each other for who they are. On this occasion I couldn't do it because I had grown up in a certain culture with certain ideals and was very resistant to changing my mindset. I recognised after that, that I needed to be with someone more like me with shared values and expectations. The unfortunate thing was that I had to go through this situation to figure this out. I ended up breaking someone's heart which is not OK. When we begin relationships we should try our best to make sure it is a long term decision because we're dealing with human beings with feelings and emotions. Breaking a heart could potentially leave long term damage long after you've moved on which could affect that person's future relations and ability to trust anyone else again. It is one of the most selfish things that so many people, particularly a lot of men, are very used to doing, and for some reason we seldom look back to think about the effects of our actions. I felt so bad when I realised that this is indeed what I had done, and I determined never to have a failed relationship ever again. It was not the way I wanted to live my life or anything I ever wanted to be known for.

There is of course one person in particular that has been mentioned in quite a few chapters in this book and now needs a very special mention. This of course is Barbara… the poet. Barbara, who I met all those years ago, is now my "significant other". So what happened? Well, after those crazy days in my second year when I had very immaturely ended what seemed to be a blossoming relationship, we began to speak again but now simply as friends. We never confronted each other about the whole episode of me completely cutting her off and maintained a reasonably professional distance. Barbara was at times very aggressive to me during team meetings during the first few years in Elevation Networks but I never actually made the link between her abruptness and the potential of her still being quite angry about my previous behaviour. This was of course a link that I should have made and was indeed the case to a large extent. The thought of her and me being together barely crossed my mind for years. I had a few relationships that never worked out and was just doing fine. Looking back, it was quite strange to see that Barbara was the only person involved in some of the most significant moments of my life.

She was indeed there at the first Elevation event when we had a poetry and jazz night. I must say that after the first EN team meeting all those years ago she first told me that she never wanted to be a part of the team but I convinced her to carry on. She attended the first ever corporate meeting for Elevation Networks, and spoke very well at the launch event. When I had decided to become a member of the Conservative Party, Barbara was first quite against the idea, but surprisingly changed her mind when she accompanied me to the launch of the UK Power List of the most influential black people. I was the youngest person to feature in the publications within their up and comings section, and they had given me two tickets to attend a reception with the then Prime Minister, Gordon Brown.

For some reason I chose to take Barbara, much to the dismay of some of the people in the team who wanted to come. Once Gordon Brown had finished his speech, Barbara turned to me and said that she had made her mind up about which political party she would now pledge her allegiance. Mr Brown had actually spoken quite well and so I was very surprised when she said she was now a Conservative. She then accompanied me to subsequent meetings and was sponsored by my church, along with myself, to do the 10 month course with the Conservative Christian Fellowship. She has also been a youth leader in my church with me. There were countless other significant moments when Barbara was with me on this journey called life, and I guess it took me years to realise that the lady that had felt like my soul mate all those years ago was indeed just that.

So how did we end up together? I went on an international development mission with some of the men in my church during the summer of 2010. We were supporting a charity called Habitat for Humanity and travelled to Romania where we were building houses. On the way there, I started to think about my life and who I would end up marrying. Barbara came to the mind and I thought that she could be the one but I wasn't too sure. As the days went on the thoughts started getting stronger and stronger, and on one of the nights I decided to have a conversation with her via Blackberry messenger. I didn't know too much about her private life so I wanted to find a way to ask her if she was with anyone.

We started a conversation and got down to the fact that there was no one particular in her life. When I got back from Romania it was time for my church's annual summer youth retreat and of course Barbara was one of the other leaders. So I took it as an opportunity really to exam whether or not I wanted to be with her. I saw sides to her that I had never seen before as she was really coming out of her shell, dancing and doing some really silly things. It showed me that she had balance and wasn't just this serious young lady which was her reputation at the time.

The turning point came during one of the lunch times. I had been messing about with one of the other leaders and they got a bit irritated and threw water over me. I was in complete shock and everyone kind of froze in shock too. Barbara was the only one who decided to go to grab some tissue to help me out. Whilst everyone else was stagnant, I was thinking that Barbara had shown that she actually cared for me. That was the moment when I decided that she was the one for me, and a few days later I made my feelings very clear.

Barbara of course was initially very scared and did not want to be another victim of a failed relationship, but eventually we got through the various apprehensions and the rest is history. We married at the famous Mission Inn which is situated in Riverside in California. Presidents Reagan and Nixon are amongst the many high profile people that have chosen to be married at the Mission Inn, and it was an experience that I'll treasure for the rest of my life.

We were upgraded to the Presidential suite on the evening of our wedding, and the weather was so amazing. To be in another country with close family and friends was so special, and of course we explored Los Angeles before the big day. We stayed on in Riverside for a few days after the wedding and really enjoyed the peace and quiet that comes with being alone for a little while. It was a bit difficult not to think about work, but if there was ever a place that I will treasure in my heart for the rest of my life (besides the borough of Barnet of course), it would be the Mission Inn, Riverside, California.

Barbara is the only lady that fully understands who I am and what I am to represent. She is a leader within her own right and someone that I know who has the strength to stand by me during what may be many tough times ahead. We share the same passions, have similar backgrounds, and complement each other in many ways. I do not regret the time it took for me in particular to wake up to these facts as I had to grow up a lot over those subsequent years. I'm just happy that when I eventually woke up she was still there and was able to accept that although I had made many mistakes, I was still the young man who she had bought into all those years ago. She knew and still knows the great vision that is enshrined in my heart and there is absolutely no one else in the world so perfect for me. Barbara isn't perfect but she's perfect for me. What is so special about Barbara is that she can in many ways be considered my equal. I do not need to worry about her ever feeling any sense of inferiority which in the past has affected some of my previous relationships. She is in fact a lot brighter than me and is able to do things that I would rather not begin to face.

A preacher once said that the person you will marry will more likely than not be someone from your own neighbourhood. He meant that it is likely that someone within close proximity to you will be the person that you will spend the rest of your life with. At first I thought that this wasn't the case, and I was very against being with someone from the same church as me. I wouldn't need to deal with any consequences if the relationship never worked out. I think the wise preacher was probably very correct and most of us are looking for something that has probably been around us the whole time. As a Christian, I'd of course say that you should pray for God to send you the person of your dreams, and I'd also advise people to avoid making too many mistakes. Every failed relationship is indeed a failure and no failure is OK. It's something that should be avoided at all costs and of course learnt from if not avoided. As a friend of mine once commented, we shouldn't kiss too many frogs before we find our prince... or princess.

This brings me nicely onto the other key set of relationships in my life that has been a part of my overall growth, and that is my family. I am from a very big family with four siblings with the same mother and father, and a baby sister with the same mother but a different father. My own Father also has a number of other children which makes for a very big immediate family. What my family has added to me is quite simply a richness of experiences that I will never forget. Thankfully, my Mother decided to relocate to Barnet when we returned from Nigeria when I was six years old.

I've basically lived there all of the years since then and as a result I have come to call it the best place in the world. Most people laugh or are very confused when I say this but deep down I recognise just how good this area has been to my family and me. We went to very good schools, lived in very safe areas, and engaged with some very good people. There were moments when both of our parents were not in the country, and if we had lived in another area, the potential for our lives to have turned out very differently would have been high.

I think about my little brother and myself in particular and recognise that we could have easily become very influenced by our surroundings with no parental supervision and the results could have been disastrous. I am very grateful for the excellent area and will continue to call it the best place in the world. It is my haven and many times when I've had very busy activities, I'm very happy to come back to the London Borough of Barnet to get some rest. My Mother has tried hard to support what is a very large family by any stretch of the imagination. Growing up in a single parent household has really made me see that it should never be seen as a credible ideal. Living in Barnet along with the support of places like our church has meant that my family has managed to turn out very well. But many families do not have the same favourable aspects to their life and have to often suffer the consequences. Absent fathers in particular leave economic, emotional, and relational scars on their children, often for life, and something needs to be done about it. I often look at some of my siblings and see that they have suffered as a result of not having a father figure in their lives. I am of course the oldest boy in my immediate family, but I'm also the fourth child and so it was very difficult for me to even imagine how to go about being the man of any house.

There were times when I really wanted to do more for my family but really couldn't, which made me feel quite power-less. My little brother, Philip, is someone who maybe I failed while he was growing up. He certainly always looked up to me, and he is now a very large body builder because I was quite stocky in my school days, believe it or not. He wanted to be like me and started to go to the gym a lot. Whilst I gave up the dream at university, he actually stepped up his training once he started at Essex University. I love him very dearly and think that now that we are a bit older our relationship has become a lot closer. I felt growing up that I somehow needed to fill the void left by our Father. The truth is of course that this should never have been a responsibility of mine and in an ideal world the family unit would have been more stable.

We grew up in a good area but were certainly not well-to-do, and as a result it took a long time to break out of the poverty trap. My elder sisters have all done particularly well in their respective careers and studies, but as a young man in the house there has been a lot of personal pressure put on me to deliver. Deciding to become an entrepreneur and political figure has not always been the most supported choice, and there were countless times when family members would question whether or not I was making the right decision in doing this. It was clearly not bringing in the money during the first few years as a graduate and they wanted me to contribute sooner rather than later to the upkeep of the house.

They also cared about my future of course, and did not want to see someone with so much promise not realise his potential, and they didn't want me to live a life of regrets in the years ahead because I did not get to where I wanted. It was an added pressure that I faced once I left university and certainly added to the stress related health problems that I would have in the first few years after graduating. I tried my best to keep going despite opposition and at different times they would all say how proud they were when they'd either attend one of my events or see me in a newspaper or publication. I was making the family proud and they were very happy to see me pushing ahead, but they just wanted me to make a little more money whilst doing the great work. I really love my family and the many different characters that we have in it. Family is the one group of people you can't choose and should be amongst the very few people that should be by your side come rain or shine.

In many respects choosing to be an entrepreneur or being involved in something like politics takes a lot of faith. As it was once described in the Bible, 'faith is the substance of things hoped for, the evidence of things not seen'. It is a tool that can be used by anyone to facilitate an action, but my own personal faith journey of course is based on my Christian faith. Leaving university has certainly helped to take my faith into new dimensions. There were times when I had nothing but had to keep going with the hope that something would come.

I remember a particular time when I had to attend a lunch meeting but only had enough money to for transport there and back. I went there knowing that I couldn't pay but thought that somehow I would get through it. Thankfully the person I went to meet offered to pay, which was the saving grace because we had actually ended up in a Michelin starred restaurant. There were times after university when I barely had any paid work but just kept chasing the dream of helping other people to push on in life.

I refused to claim a benefit of any kind at any point in my journey because I never wanted it to be something that would hinder my own journey in the future. I didn't want the State to feel it could somehow compromise my ability to tell my journey of faith in regards to how I battled adversity to get to some high office. I have really come to value the potential of faith communities to be active particularly in respect of providing for a family.

My church is my second family, and is a place where I feel very at home. I go there for encouragement, advice, guidance, love, relationship, support, and so many other valuable things that I couldn't find anywhere else so freely and available. Growing up without living with my Father has meant that the church is really where I learnt how to be a man. Watching how the pastors and others treated their wives and listening to the various sermons on how to have very rich relationships has been an absolute blessing. This isn't simply limited to the work in my own church. Barbara and I have been on a pre- marriage course at Holy Trinity Brompton where we were given excellent insight into the many things that we will need to know in regards to how to keep our relationship strong in the years ahead. It is my hope that in the years ahead the church will not become isolated but will instead be known for the two greatest commandments of its faith: love God and love thy neighbour. It is those two commandments that demonstrate the fact that faith in God should not be something that threatens people, but it should instead be a source of hope and comfort for humanity as a whole. For if there are a people that have love at the centre of their ultimate ambition then the world certainly has a place where they can say that there is still some good.

It was this same love that encouraged the educating of young people before education was even seen as right and not a privilege by the British government. Up until the late 19th century the church was responsible for educating many young people and it continues to do so in many respects today. Christians all across developing nations are still providing many with care where no one else seems to be. Whether it's in remote villages where there is a Christian Mission Society (CMS) member providing a free healthcare service or school for the locals, or whether it is one of the many churches with their own activities across the world, the Christian faith continues to be a vehicle for love even though many in the western world would like to argue otherwise.

I for one will hope to be a voice for the church in the years ahead when we can expect to see even more voices rise up in opposition to the faith. My personal relationship with God through my Christian faith has continued to be a key part of my journey through various ups and downs, and it is something that I hope will continue to carry me as I carry on to press on towards the goal God has given me.

The many relationships that I've had over the years have without a doubt helped to shape who I am today. The people in this chapter each have had a part to play in the successes that I've managed to achieve over the years and for this I am eternally grateful. I guess the truth is that without people in our lives we're merely just living. Real richness is in the people that you can call on in your hour of need and not simply the money in your bank account. Of course there have been many times when I have felt alone, particularly when I've been in leadership positions where I've been quite isolated. Thankfully, during many of these moments I've had mentors who have given me the advice that I've needed to get through any challenges. My relationship with myself is also something that has been important to pushing on in the midst of many setbacks and adversities. I have had to tell myself that what I am doing is the right thing to do at times when most people around me maybe thought the opposite.

In my loneliest moments when I've been alone with my tears, feeling like I was ready to give up, I've had to remember the people who were waiting for me to succeed. Those young people I mentor, the people who are reading about me in various publications, and the people who have no idea who I am, will one day know that it is possible to make their dreams a reality because I've managed to do it too. I have been privileged to open many doors that people thought were shut to certain types of people, and as a result many people have taken it as permission for them to do the same thing. This is the one thing that continues to motivate me to keep on going and keep on pressing forward towards the goal.

Student politics was my first journey, then I moved into business, but of course the expected end of this journey is politics. This is the place where I hope one day to show the world that all things are possible, and this is where I hope to make the biggest difference. I need to be able to show everyone that politics is relevant to everyone and anyone can participate within the various power structures.

Chapter 9

Building A Brand & Network

One of the early lessons that I learnt when trying to achieve success in business, and later in politics, was that I needed to build a very strong brand and network if I was to give myself any chance of reaching the top. When setting up Elevation Networks, it was very clear that the other businesses in the market were established because they had been founded by people in the very industries that they wished to engage. The market leaders had been founded by bankers and thus found it very easy to attract investment banks as partners. We, on the other hand, were just students with a dream, and therefore I needed to build a strong personal profile in order for people to buy into what we were selling.

The same applied to politics. I had not studied Politics, Philosophy, and Economics (PPE) at Oxford or Cambridge, and never even studied at a Russell Group University. In fact, I had never studied politics full stop. I was not political class material by those standards, and was very sure that I did not want simply to be given any positions without merit. I wanted to get to the political top, but in a way that no one could doubt the value that I had and my hard work. People in politics needed to respect that I had just as much of a right to be at the top as anyone else, and no one would have to feel as if they were doing me any favours.

I guess the first way that my personal brand was being built was through my various positions in student politics. In being the President of the largest society on campus, I automatically became well known both inside and outside of my university. I then became the Vice-President of my Union, which of course meant that I represented 14,000 students. This again helped to enhance my own personal brand, and it was very useful when approaching various potential stake-holders in business and politics.

I've seen many students who have been very active on campus whilst studying that end up not really pushing on after university. They either do not end up at the job that they've dreamt of or maybe end up very slow off the tracks after graduation. Of course there are also some great success stories, like my good friend Marsha. She was on my committee when I was President of the African & Caribbean Society, and was a committee member of the Entrepreneur Society during her final year of university. She went on to work at leading a consultancy firm, Accenture, and by 25 was Assistant Director at UBS, one of the largest investment banks in the world. The key to her success, and one of the most important things to appreciate in life, is that she always had the end in mind. Whilst she focused greatly on becoming a great student, and adding value to the experiences of her fellow students on campus, Marsha also ensured that she was positioning herself for the next level. This is a balancing act that most students simply do not manage to get right.

In politics, it's similar to having the right policies for the current climate whilst also anticipating the next election. In business, it's serving your current customers whilst under-standing where the company will need to be in a few years time in line with market changes. Most of us focus so much on the present that we fail to be one step ahead in preparing for the medium to long term future. Of course others are far too preoccupied with the future to embrace the present. Personal branding is about striking the balance, selecting places where you would like to add value now, whilst also being very aware of what is needed of you for your next chapter. My future was in business and politics, so I knew that I needed to demonstrate my ability to engage with both before I moved on. This is why it was very important to launch my first company whilst still at university, and was also why it made a lot of sense to be involved in student politics.

My plan was to make sure that I had enough business experience before entering politics. I didn't want people to label me a career politician, so I wanted to become successful in building an enterprise before I pushed on. In order to build a credible brand, I decided that I would work with the world's leading brands first, with the hope that this would allow the organisation to be seen as a strong company to work with. So our first corporate partners were an investment bank, this was followed by us working with the likes of IBM, HSBC, and many others. When we were pitching to other companies, we had a very strong track record to draw on, and we could also position ourselves as a very professional going concern because of our experience, and not just a bunch of students.

It also meant that once we diversified into delivering public sector contracts, we had a track record that was a bit unique compared to others. We could say that we had links to corporate brands, and had an offering that was a lot more creative. I'd go to pitch to business development departments and they would genuinely be fascinated by this youth-led organisation that had such strong links to industries. Indeed, this was the main reason that most of them bought into what we were doing. We certainly never had the financial history that you would need at times to justify bidding for large contracts.

Elevation Networks was my first venture, but I always knew that it was a venture with a social conscious, and something that would be of a charitable nature. Its objectives were pure as we wanted to help make young people more competitive at a time when unemployment amongst young people was such a great epidemic across the world. I also felt that for this organisation truly to grow, I needed to become a brand that was also well respected within the industry. So my own personal brand needed to grow, and for this to happen, I needed to be recognised within my field.

The first stage of this was really an accident. In 2008 I was featured in the UK Power List of most influential black people as one of their 'Up and Coming' individuals. Being featured in such a prestigious publication had meant that people were now looking at me as someone with quite large social capital. It also led to me attending my first engagement in Downing Street, and me mixing with some of the most influential people in the country for the first time. Being featured in the publication helped to give our work a lot exposure for the first time. This is of course one of the biggest problems many people and organisations face, not knowing how to let people hear about the great work that they are doing. I've found that in the Third Sector in particular, many charities and not-for-profit companies find it very hard to make people aware of their great work. Many small companies find it hard to develop a strong communication strategy, and feel they can't justify spending money on paying experts. I would recommend attending a free training course around developing a strong communication strategy as well as seriously considering paying experts to support this.

In 2010 I was featured in the new Future Leaders supplement of the Power List, and then again in 2011 I was identified as a Top 10 Future Leaders in the UK by the Power List. I was also featured by Rare Recruitment as a Rare Rising Star. My stock began to rise, and people started to hear about the work of Elevation Networks. I was also appeared regularly in my local newspapers, and was featured in the leading ethnic minority newspaper, The Voice. There were also various faith magazines, including Keep the Faith, and over the years I have been mentioned in other publications. There have also been various television and radio programmes, including BBC News. The more my personal brand grew, the more doors were opened for me to champion the things that I was most passionate about. People were no longer looking at us as just a bunch of students, we were now being taken very seriously. I always tell people, 'what use is treasure if it is at the bottom of the sea'. In the same respect, if people do not know the work you are doing, it is very difficult to benefit from sustainable growth, and is therefore difficult to fulfil your objectives.

As well as being recognised in various publications, I've also been fortunate to win several awards. I received the Barclays Business Enterprise Award, at the Spirit of London

Award (SOLA) ceremony in the Royal Albert Hall. This was something very special to me, because the awards were founded in honour of the late Damilola Taylor. The award was presented to me by the co-founder of Lastminute.com which was quite cool. I've gone on to become co-chairman of the SOLA Select Committee, and now support the strategy for what are the largest youth awards in the UK. I was also the first ever person to win the Young Star of Enterprise Award at the Growing Business award ceremony in association with CBI and Real Business Magazine.

2011 also saw me nominated for a Black Youth Achieve-ment Award, and I was named a top three role model in the UK by Aimway International Plc. Awards are not just a good way to enhance one's brand, but they are also a great way to meet new people. Ceremonies usually have very distin-guished guests, and those nominated are all very well accom-plished in their own right. It's a great place to network, something I will touch on later in this chapter. Awards of course help to recognise the hard work that has been done when no one was watching, and though an individual picks up the award, it is really a way of recognising the efforts of a great team around them. I wouldn't be anything today if it wasn't for the great people that I have had around me over the years.

Another aspect of building a personal brand that I will touch on is probably the most important to me. Before I ran for President back in 2006 for a society on my campus, I wrote articles that helped to convey my message to the world. It was my way of demonstrating what I was passionate about, and was also an opportunity for me to stimulate and engage with rich debate. This was what helped me to build credibility amongst student voters before I ever put myself forward to be elected, and it remains a powerful way of engaging with a respective audience.

Soon after I felt that it was the right time to get more involved in politics and I realised that writing would be the best way for me to engage a new audience. I began to write articles around topics I was particularly passionate about, and, of course, with nowhere to put them, they mostly ended up on Facebook. I started to read Conservative Home, and being entrepreneurial I was very keen to try to get my pieces onto the website. Initially it was quite hard because I couldn't manage to get in contact with them. I did eventually get put in touch with the editor of ConHome, Paul Goodman. He was very helpful, and this opened me up to a potential conversation with my new political audience.

I made the decision to focus my writing on trying to articulate arguments for groups that maybe never had a significant voice within Conservative circles. This was not just ethnic minorities, but also young people and faith communities. I wanted to demonstrate what these communities were collectively thinking about in regards to certain policy areas and how the party should be engaging with them. I then went on to write for the Tory Reform Group (TRG), and then as a blogger for Huffington Post. My articles would not only spark great debate, but also galvanised support from people who agreed with what I was saying.

The beauty of platforms like Conservative Home is that activists at every level read it, and as a result you are able to share your ideas with people at the very top. There have been occasions when I have heard Ministers and fellow political commentators quote something that I had written. Eventually I wanted to take more control of my personal brand, and so decided that I would set up my own website. This would mean that when anyone searched for me online or for things that I was passionate about, they would engage with something that I could control, as opposed to whatever came up on a search engine. So I set up my own website, www.samuelkasumu.co.uk. The more I wrote articles the more my website went up in search engines, until it was ranked top when people searched for me.

Managing my own personal brand has been something that I've grown to understand is vital when attempting to become successful, especially if you're starting in a place a bit behind some of the people you're competing with. I needed to open doors for myself, and therefore I needed to build a brand strong enough to have value in the eyes of people who mattered. This also meant that I needed somehow to build a network that was very strong.

A network of course is simply relationships that are of value to both parties. I wanted people to feel that I could add value to them, as well as people to feel they could potentially add value to me. My first point of call was the people who were within my immediate environment. So my first two mentors were a member of my church congregation and a pastor in my church. The mentor from my congregation re-emphasised the need for a strong vision, mission, and strategic objectives. With his help I was able to narrow my focus and have a clear plan for what it was that I wanted to achieve. I was able therefore to be very selective with the projects that I took on, and was able to create a clear plan for my business. The member of the pastoral team at my church ensured that I was always grounded. He was very clear that I should always strive to do the right thing, and to act with the utmost integrity. At times of great crisis, where I simply did not know which direction to take, the pastor would always seem to have the right thing to say at the right moment.

It was also very clear to me that I also needed to be around people who shared the same drive to fulfil their potential, and in that respect I became very selective about the people that I associated with on a daily basis. Some of the people who were part of my past had to be cut off, which was quite difficult but essential if I was going to make it to the top.

My ambitions were, and still are, not just about personal fulfilment, but were also about showing people that it was possible to have the odds stacked against you and yet to be a great success. For this reason it was essential that I made any personal sacrifice necessary, which meant being very conscious of whom I associated with. I also realised that arguably the most important piece of my network jigsaw was the people coming up after me. I needed to find people who had great potential, and who I could teach everything that I had learnt to date. Not only would it mean that there was a new generation of leaders being developed for the future, but it also meant that I would have a group of loyal people that I could count on in the future.

I therefore concluded that in life you must have people that fit into the following three categories: 1) mentors that are wise in various areas 2) people with the same drive and ambition, and 3) people you can teach. It was my intention to add value to every one of those three types of people, and never to be at a place where people felt like I was just maintaining a relationship with them to take from them. It is my view that relationships that are always one directional seldom last because people will inevitably get tired of being used. A successful relationship is always a two way street.

Starting from scratch when building a network can sometimes be very hard and for people who find it difficult, I have some advice. I'd recommend that like me, you first start by utilising the people immediately around you. This could be people on your campus, in your church, your community, or at work. Everyone in life has a gift or talent and the potential to be someone special in life, but most of us are just too busy or insensitive to realise the value of others. We're always looking for the people with the flashy titles as opposed to appreciating those who are just as special.

To continue the growth of my network, I started to approach people using a number of techniques. The first, and most effective at the time, was through referrals. People who liked the work that we were doing at Elevation Networks, or who simply bought into my passion and drive, would put me in touch with their contacts. This was much more productive than sending a cold email to people we had never met before, and resulted in establishing new relationships. I sent out cold emails, but when I did, it was targeted. I'd research organisations that were potential partners, and would target specific departments that would be useful.

For example, within the welfare to work industry, I made sure that I contacted people in business development departments, as they would be the ones tasked with writing bids that ultimately brought in money for the firm. I knew that if I spoke to the people who handled partnerships, they'd be less likely to have access to budgets and as a result would be more focused on us doing work for free. With graduate recruitment divisions, I looked for people who worked on diversity initiatives. In politics, I made sure to target MP's who were not cabinet members. This was because I knew they would be more likely to read their own emails, and would also be keener to meet new people who could benefit their own political ambitions and priorities.

Of course, most politicians in opposition or without a portfolio have the opportunity to set their own agendas, and for me this was much more productive than chasing a Minister who would be less flexible. My logic was also that MPs that are yet to reach the pinnacle of their career would be more likely to remember and trust you if they knew you before they were elevated. So I always looked to identify people who I could add value to on their journey up and who would be directly interested in growing a relationship to suit their immediate priorities. This is one of the secrets of how I've managed to become one of the most connected people of my age.

When I contacted people via email to engage with them for the first time, there were key things that I ensured made up the message. The first thing was to make sure the email was as straight to the point and short as possible, with enough content to make the person interested. This is a skill that I became better at over time. I would throw in some figures to make sure people saw that I had a very large backing behind me, and represented a large group. I also made sure that I name dropped whenever I could.

For example, if I emailed an organisation, I would list a number of organisations that we had worked with in the past, and if it was a politician, I'd name drop other Members of Parliament who were my mentors. The email would thus show that I was a credible person to engage with and that the person's peers placed me in high enough regard to be of value. I would of course end each email would a very brief call to action. I would say, 'please let me know a convenient time to meet', or, 'it would be great to discuss possible opportunities for partnership'. I very seldom wanted anyone to believe they were simply meeting a young person to help out. I may have run a not -for-profit organisation, but I certainly was not prepared to be a charity case by any stretch of anyone's imagination. Each email was always more about what I could say that would appeal to the person I was communicating with, and less about what it was that I wanted.

In more recent times, I have had staff available to dedicate time to engaging potential partners and stakeholders. The team do extensive research into the many different types of people with whom we hope to engage. We also now use the phone directly to contact companies and to get names of people when we have found it difficult to source contacts.

We have social networking tools that we now use to engage people, including LinkedIn and Facebook. Personally, the most effective tool that I have been using to engage potential contacts is Twitter. It has allowed me to speak directly with members of the press, business figures, and politicians in ways that years ago could never have been imagined. I have managed to use Twitter to great extents, with it even resulting in one of our projects reaching the front page of the Independent Newspaper as a result. If you use Twitter right, and you engage with the right people (not just celebrities), the benefits are well and truly endless. It's the most productive social media tool out there.

Of course, once you make the initial connection the next challenge is ensuring that you make a good impression at your first meeting. You must be able to impress the person, whilst making sure you don't come across as arrogant. The first meeting is your opportunity to show people that you are worth communicating with again, and of course the first impression is the most important impression. It has never been easier to prepare for a first meeting with search engines helping to bring up vital information. I normally Google everyone that I'm about to meet, and also see what the latest engagement with them has been via social media. I look at their history, and usually have some questions for them to show that I am interested in what they do.

Hopefully after making a good first impression, I subscribe to the rule of contacting anyone that I meet within 24 hours of meeting with them to thank them for their time. I usually break this rule if I want to prepare for a follow up, or if I am no longer interested in having a relationship with them because of what I found out during our first meeting. Networking is about relationships where both groups add value to each other. I genuinely believe that if I cannot add any value as part of a relationship, it will be difficult to maintain it. I'm also very averse to connecting with people who feel like they are better than me or behave like they're doing me a favour. I avoid people like that, and in the past have been quite ruthless in avoiding people who have a chip on their shoulder.

I must also say that most of the people who I have developed relationships with are quite busy, and therefore the last thing they need is for someone to be constantly sending emails or asking for things. In that respect, I've ensured that I am careful when I contact people.

My latest networking innovation is a bi-monthly update. This is the way people can know what I'm up to and when I do connect with them, I'm not a stranger. At the same time, an update every other month is not too often, and does not become spam in anyone's mailbox. My updates are also very engaging, and people have said that they find my updates very interesting. Updates always show that I am making progress in what I'm working on, and always have some form of call to action.

I recommend that people who are trying to build their network make a list of the respective types of people they wish to engage with first, and then list the ideal people from 1 to 10. I'd then try to engage the top person on the list and work my way down. My focus on building a brand and a strong network is what has helped to open doors I couldn't have imagined as an eighteen year old starting university back in 2005.

163

For me, the challenge now is taking the work that I am doing to the next level, and making sure that I make a tangible difference to the lives of the most vulnerable in society. Maintaining my integrity is the most important thing, as this is what will ensure that both the brand and the network remain strong.

As mentioned at the beginning of this book, my journey through life has been one that has been both ordinary and extraordinary in many respects. I grew up in a single parent home, with financial struggles, and was in and out of schools until I reached university. The disruption probably meant that I could not reach my academic potential, and also meant that I was able to experience different types of community early on. All of my experiences have helped to shape my ideas today, and has led to my current personal convictions about how society should be shaped, the role of the State, and the true value that faith communities still have to play locally, nationally, and internationally.

Although I wouldn't change any of my experiences, I sometimes think that if I had been a bit stronger and wiser at particular points in my life, would I have made different choices? If I knew that education would be so important to my future, maybe I would have decided to study at Imperial College as opposed to rejecting my place there, but something tells me that I probably would have made the same choice. If I knew how important A Levels were, would I have used the same logic to pick the subjects that I chose? Probably! And if I knew that I would have ended up in East Barnet School as a result of being a rather naughty pupil, would I have improved my behaviour? Again, I very much doubt it. On this occasion hindsight has only led me to conclude that we go through the many challenges of life to make us all stronger and wiser. The journey is just as important, if not more important at times, than the destination because this is what helps to shape our character, which in turn allows us to become more productive members of society.

If there is anything that I do regret, then it is probably not working harder at certain points in my life. I feel like maybe

I could have done a lot more by this stage of my life. But then, maybe at the age of 24, I am being a bit too hard on myself. When you have a clear vision like I do, and a purpose for why you are doing it, I guess it gives you a reason to wake up in the morning. I know that my life is one that must be used in public service, and my ambition is to show young people like me across the world that they can be anything that they so desire. I want to go further in showing people that it really doesn't matter where you start in life, it's more importantly about where you finish. What is your gift to humanity, your legacy to the world, your inheritance to your children's children? How will you be remembered by the next generation?

My immediate priority now is to add value to the Conservative Party, and help to influence its thinking as we prepare for the next General Elections and beyond. I hope to be a voice for equality within the Party. I also have unfinished work to do in the world of business, and hope to grow my enterprises to becoming a large multinational concern. Emerging markets are of particular interest to me because of the great opportunity to shape things and to give birth to new ideas. Hopefully I am able to fulfil these goals before one day entering UK politics on a full time basis.

I'll end this section by mentioning the people that inspire me the most in today's world. As a Christian, my deepest inspiration must be Jesus Himself. His leadership, humility, wisdom, and selflessness are something that sets the best example for anyone who wants to make a difference in our world. I also have great respect for the great church reformer Martin Luther, and my number one guru is Martin Luther King Jnr. These are great men who chose to stand for what they believed to be right and in the best interest of the most vulnerable in society. I hope that one day, you and I, like these great men, will be able to look back and say that we were also able to be leaders of our generation.

Section 3:

My Personal Creed

Chapter 10

Conservative Challenge Ahead

Any political group in a healthy democracy must have the ambition of winning elections at the core of its thinking. This competition, in theory, should help to foster innovation when attempting to provide the best offering for the people whom it is privileged to serve. Indeed, the opportunity to govern a whole nation is partly why most get involved in politics in the first place. The difference that any politician can make will only really ever fully materialise if one has the power to bring about change. The Conservative Party is the largest party in the land based on the amount of votes it receives at elections, but current boundaries mean that it has become increasingly difficult for the party to command a parliamentary majority.

To make things more difficult for the Conservatives, current predictions anticipate that the types of people that are least likely ever to vote for them are also the same groups that are due to grow in size over the next 40 years. By 2051 it is anticipated that at least 20 percent of people in the UK will be from an ethnic minority background. Only 16 percent of all ethnic minorities voted Conservative at the last general election. Surprisingly this was actually a record figure. Those ethnic minorities who voted Conservative probably did so for one of two reasons. Either they were a part of a growing ethnic minority community who are becoming socially mobile and independently minded, or they were disillusioned with the then Labour government. Let us look at these two potential reasons carefully.

In regards to the growing socially mobile ethnic minority

community in Britain, we know that some of Labour's policies have opened up various doors that were traditionally shut to marginalised communities. For example, Labour's target of having 50% of young people attend university meant that many families now had graduates for the first time. Of course we know that a graduate is on average likely to make £100,000 more than someone that did not study at university over the course of their life. This kind of policy has helped a new ethnic minority generation of young ambitious and educated individuals to be established, an emerging middle class one could say. Labour spent millions on various activities like Aim Higher and Widening Participation in order to fulfil their bold university targets, and as a result has helped the Conservatives in some ways.

This growing educated population could now think more independently and would now question why they should automatically vote Labour. I am certain of this fact, because of course I am one of these young people. My family always voted Labour, but the more I read and observed, the more I became a dissatisfied with this idea. Members of this emerging ethnic minority middle class have managed to recognise that a lot of their values are actually more aligned with the Conservatives. I must say, however, that even when this 'Damascus Road' conversion takes place, the vast majority still cannot bring themselves to vote Conservative. It is still seen as something that just shouldn't be done. The words of their parents about how the party treated them during Thatcher's reign and beyond still echoes in their heads when they enter their polling stations. Most of these people who are socially mobile have never really lived through a Conservative government as they would have been quite young at the time. As a result, their parent's memories have been the only thing for them to draw upon when attempting to make an informed decision on which party to vote for.

The second group of people who were likely to have been part of this record breaking 16 percent that voted for the Conservatives were those who were clearly not happy with Labour. These are people who for various reasons chose to exercise a protest vote. Ethnic minority voters who feel Labour have lost the desire to represent them. There are various policy areas that we can point to where Labour lost some of their traditional voting monopoly on ethnic minority communities. They include the war in Afghanistan, failure to deal with crime within inner city areas, a lack of job opportunities, and failing to get to grips with the economy.

I think it is once again important to recognise that not everyone who was disgruntled with Labour stopped voting for them and then went on to vote Conservative. The vast majority either didn't vote, voted Labour, or voted for the Liberal Democrats. People still couldn't bring themselves to vote Conservative, even if the only realistic alternative to the Conservatives was going to be sticking with Gordon Brown. The few that decided to vote Conservative are worth focusing on at this point. For some, like my Mother, who was at the time convinced to try out this new brand of Conservative politics, now regret the decision and are currently unlikely to vote in the same way again. They feel that the Conservative Party is not doing enough to help the working classes, and are not exercising policies that are of key importance to them.

Labour is now coordinating a re-branding exercise, and seems effectively to be distancing themselves from any memory of New Labour. Not only are they doing this well, but they are also managing slowly to reposition their party as one for the working class. This of course is the socio economic group where the majority of ethnic minority communities are located.

We must also appreciate that the main centre left alternative would have been the Liberal Democrats. We know that the Liberals still maintain a consistent, relatively low, level of support through various polls. But more importantly, those who decided to vote Liberal Democrat in 2010 instead of Labour are now unlikely to repeat that decision in 2015. Tuition fees are just one of the many reasons why swing voters feel betrayed by the Liberals. Labour has benefited from the Liberals being a minority within a majority Conservative led government, and we have seen a large increase in their membership from Liberal Democrat defectors as a result since 2010.

So where does this leave the Conservative Party? Well, it is very plausible that by 2015 the economy could show positive signs of recovery, even though many economists anticipate austerity measures lasting till well after the next General Election. But in the long term, if Conservatives can ever hope to maintain power for a sustainable period of time, Cameron's rebranding agenda must go a step further. At times it has seemed as though the Party has compromised its values in order to appear more Liberal. I don't think this is helpful when trying to demonstrate a strong alternative to the other parties or when trying to maintain the Party's core support. I think there is a way to create policy that is truly Conservative, but also appeals to groups that are not traditional Tory voters.

Whilst I won't be articulating in full my ideas in this book, just like when I ran in an election for a society on my campus years ago, I will be writing articles about these ideas, and hopefully one day I'll be able to help to implement them... In the mean time, I hope you enjoy some of my thought pieces which I've put in the book to help demonstrate how my thinking has evolved over the years. Ben Harris-Quinney, the Chairman of the Bow Group, has kindly written the Afterword for this book. He is a very fine and intelligent gentleman that has been doing a fantastic job since being elected chairman of the oldest centre right think tank in the United Kingdom.

Chapter 11

Growing My Ideas

Is the Big Society failing the voluntary sector?
(Published by Huffington Post 2012)

The Prime Minister's Big Society was supposed to be the key initiative that would bring together every policy area within the Conservative Manifesto. It was an underpinning philosophy that could be used to rebuild communities, allow for the reshaping of various public services, and above all demonstrate that the Tories were able to be compassionate.

This was planned to be the legacy of David Cameron's premiership, and would make Britain a better place. But it is easy for everyone to see that from the time this 'Big Idea' was launched to the public it hasn't managed to capture the imagination of the masses. The recent revelation that one of the first Big Society Ambassadors has had to close down his charity will no doubt further harm its already tarnished brand.

Shaun Bailey was the talented and outspoken community leader that the Conservatives managed to sign up to represent a section of Britain that they continue to struggle to engage. Shaun is the founder of the now extinct charity, My Generation. He is black, from a working class background, and passionate about dealing with the issues that affect the most marginalised people within communities. Following Bailey's unsuccessful election campaign in 2010, David Cameron rewarded his loyalty and hard work by giving him the title of being one of his 'Big Society Ambassadors. He now serves as a special adviser to the Prime Minister's office.

Unfortunately he has since had to close down his charity which he set up to help young people within poor areas.

The mission of My Generation is completely in line with what the Big Society stands for, but this sad loss to communities within Hammersmith may actually be the most important thing that Shaun Bailey does as a former Big Society Ambassador. In having to close down his own charity, Shaun has demonstrated to the government and to those with similar organisations that he indeed understands and shares similar challenges to most voluntary groups in the UK today.

There is no doubt that funding for community groups has arguably always been the key challenge that they face when delivering much needed support to their service users. However, we are in an economic crisis where funding is increasingly smaller and harder to come across. During the Labour years we saw money being given out in larger proportions through local and national government schemes, as well as a larger availability of grants. But in recent times funding for things like Children and Young People Services has been close to being wiped out by local council's as they have no statutory obligation to deliver such activities. Other lifelines like the Future Jobs Fund have been scrapped, which has meant that many voluntary sector organisations can no longer benefit from the use of extra staff that is funded by the government. So the voluntary sector faces big challenges going forward and the long term survival of many of these organisations is something that simply cannot be guaranteed. Some would view this all as a major tragedy, but I see this more as an opportunity to create a solution that is fit for purpose. Like a game of chess, with the opponent thinking the game is almost over, the Big Society may yet still have one more move.

The government must now look at ways of reshaping the voluntary sector to ensure that it allows people that are passionate about society not to be lost because of economic difficulty. They should set up Big Society Academies that train up community leaders and gives them the skills to identify and engage with the funding areas that still exist, as well as other key skills. This training should be delivered by corporate partners on a pro bono basis. Many community leaders do not have the in-depth knowledge of how to effectively run a going concern and are simply people that care for their communities. There passion must be harnessed and supported with training and support from experts from various fields. I can certainly envision major corporations donating their time for free to train large groups of voluntary sector staff and volunteers. Although some are already doing this, the scale must be increased. This would no doubt be something that helps to enhance their brand from a Corporate Social Responsibility (CSR) perspective.

There are a number of different activities that local and national governments still fund, but to be able to receive any money will require many organisations to become a bit more entrepreneurial. Things like the National Citizen Service gives out funding of over £1000 for every young person that engages with the scheme. This is a lot of money, but at the moment only very large organisations like the Princes Trust and V-Inspired seem to be winning such contracts. So a major issue is how smaller voluntary groups can participate in the delivery of such schemes in larger proportions. There are a few success stories of this happening, but not nearly as much as would be needed to demonstrate success in line with Big Society aspirations.

Voluntary groups will need to partner with larger organisations if they simply do not have the capacity to survive by themselves, and others will have to seriously consider the possibility of merging. The government must do its part in revolutionising the voluntary sector without taking it over. They should eventually make a fund available for community groups with fewer strings attached and less bureaucracy in the application stage. Cameron must also find a way for people that are involved in the voluntary sector to secure paid work. It must be said that Bailey's role as an ambassador was unpaid and he therefore represented many community leaders that are doing the work that most people believe they are too busy to do, and is sacrificing his own time without being fairly remunerated. There must also be targeted funding available for communities to create solutions where there are gaps in public services due to the limited funding available at this current time.

The Big Society still has the potential to empower us all to further engage with our own communities. But this will only happen when the government supports those that have been doing Big Society things way before it was a Big Idea. The voluntary sector must not be lost whilst other people with no passion for their communities continue to be given a stay of economic execution. More support is needed, more engagement is essential, and more of a collective strategy must be announced if we are to avoid too many more stories like Shaun Bailey's My Generation.

The Injustice in Current Social Mobility Policy
(Published in Tory Reform Group Social Mobility Pamphlet 2012)

The opening words of the new social mobility report launched by the All Party Parliamentary Group on this topic area states that the report was produced to "discuss and promote the cause of social mobility; to raise issues of concern and help inform policy makers and formers". Whilst the above objectives are certainly admirable, I guess it also helps to highlight the fact that the UK has not progressed as effectively as we all would have liked in regards to creating a fairer platform for all groups to push on in life. Indeed the gap between the rich and the poor had widened over the 13 years of Labour government. Whilst this current coalition is only in its second year, we remain in economically hard times with very high levels of unemployment. Upon this backdrop we must ask ourselves whether or not there is truly an appetite to get Britain socially mobile amongst those who have power. There is a great difference between the words appetite and desire. One can live with a desire to have something, but an appetite is a lot harder to ignore.

Conservatives by very nature believe in individual responsibility, minimal intervention from the state, and of course freedom to realise ones potential. We believe that everyone in our country should have the opportunity to fulfil their true potential as this is the best way for us to remain competitive within an in increasingly globalized world. But where have we gone wrong? Why is it that in one of the richest countries in the world, with such excellent intellectual institutions, and billions of pounds being spent on providing a plethora of services, we still do not have social outcomes that would make us all far more comfortable? Day after day, week after week, our young people are becoming less and less competitive both on a domestic and global level. We are ranked 17th for reading and 24th for maths in the world rankings on education. Our education system simply isn't giving us the result's that we need which is why Michael Gove must continue with his radical shake up. But our education budget for this fiscal year is £89.5 billion, so no one can really say a lack of funding is the problem. We simply are not currently competitive, and the groups that are disproportionately under achieving have been clearly identified for many years now. Even the so called low skilled jobs are being taken up by economic migrants from Europe. We've had the famous case of Prêt a Manger employing high levels of non UK citizens, and Chris Grayling recently encouraging employers to 'higher a hoodie'. I'd be interested to know how many of these 'hoodies' were employed over at DWP.

So we have very difficult problems on every level, and the findings from this report are almost identical to the findings of a report we recently launched in Parliament titled; Race to the Top. This report was launched in partnership with business services firm Deloitte. It focused on the experiences of black students within Higher Education, and their outlook on employment as a result. We found that black students are three times more likely to be unemployed upon graduation than white students, and that they were likely to earn 9% less after 5 years doing the same work. We also found that 60% of black students anticipated experiencing some form of discrimination when trying to progress in their careers. I guess the most interesting finding of the report for me was that students felt that government and policy careers were the most discriminatory to break into. Of course this was a study focusing on one particular community within the UK, but for me it made me realise one thing; that as a Conservative my party has really ignored a whole section of society and swift action must be taken.

Social mobility is a phrase that we can interchange with justice. Martin Luther King Jnr once said that 'injustice anywhere is a threat to justice everywhere' and I guess he was right in the sense that you cannot ignore one groups experiences and believe that as a collective community we can truly reach our full potential. The government simply has no policy when it comes to dealing with ethnic minority communities and the equality challenges that they face. The Conservatives in particular have ignored the need to look at these groups for fear that this would somehow be a conversation too uncomfortable to have. But the facts are that people from ethnic minority backgrounds tend to live in large communities where they have unique challenges. For example, there are large Pakistani communities in the North East, and we only need to look at the Bradford West by-election to hear their cry for help. African & Caribbean communities are heavily concentrated within inner city areas, and 50% of the young people from this background are unemployed. This is in contrast to the national average of 20%.

Tower Hamlets has a large Bangladeshi community with huge academic and economic challenges, and 25% of Leicester is of Indian heritage. These are communities that have a unique cultural experience whether we like it or not, and have challenges that cannot be ignored. Not only is acknowledging this the right thing to do, but it is the only way that Conservatives will be able to command a majority in the future. Currently in the UK, 1 in 4 students in Primary school are from an ethnic minority background. These are our future voters of tomorrow, who currently have parents that do not vote Conservative. We only managed to get 16% of the ethnic minority vote in 2010, with many of the marginal seats that we lost having very large ethnic communities. If these groups exist with such disparities in regards to their academic and economic outcomes, then these groups must be considered when pushing ahead with creating any social mobility policies. They simply cannot be ignored, because their size and potential benefits to our country in the longer term could be enormous. For in tomorrow's global world, having UK citizens with dual heritage could only add more value as we seek to win more international business, and to build new relationships in emerging markets.

I guess the question is where do we go from here? Some would argue that the challenges that ethnic minority communities face are purely down to class, but evidence has shown that even when we account for class there remain challenges like institutional racism and unconscious bias. We also know that the government has an integration strategy, but people that are second, third, and sometimes fourth generation UK citizens simply cannot relate to an idea of being 'integrated'. Frankly, this could be seen as an insult. So we must now look at policies that speak directly to some of the problems that have been highlighted above. I would call on the government to have an independent review into the specific challenges that ethnic minorities face, and to identify where these issue can be seen as class related, but also where there is a very clear race related problem. The main policy areas that must be considered are education, employment, crime, business, and public life. We need to know why it is that a Chinese student performs better than all communities at school and Further Education level, but is less likely to get a first class degree than a white student at university, and has significantly lower employment outcomes. We also need to know what role geographic location plays in economic mobility, and how we can encourage the next generation of ethnic minority young people to think outside of inner city areas. Simply throwing money at situations is a tried and failed response to the various inequalities that we continue to face today, but to ignore these issues is something that we simply cannot afford to do.

My final thought is about our nation's future. We are a country that has such a rich history. We have managed to maintain a presence on the world stage even though our size and limited natural resources has meant that in many ways we have punched above our weight. But tomorrow's world is something that we must all recognise will bring a very different landscape. India, Nigeria, Bangladesh, and of course China, are amongst economies that are growing at alarming rates. These are nations that all once looked to, and relied heavily on, Great Britain for assistance from a development perspective. And whilst we of course remain in a position to help these nations on their way to economic development, we have to realise that they will one day all be countries that are powerful giants because of their shear potential. They have an abundance of resources, growing human capital, and increasing intellectual property. How will Britain remain at the cutting edge and still relevant for years to come on the world stage? Well, the answer is very simple. These very communities that are suffering from social mobility barriers in the UK are the very same people that have the potential to keep our significance to tomorrow's super powers. For indeed if we get them socially mobile, ethnic minority communities have the potential to become one of our strongest assets as a nation.

The Power of Perception
(Written Early 2006 Aged 18)

People's perceptions are such a powerful tool, which is why the media, the government and large corporations invest time and finance in controlling our perceptions, in order to manipulate how we function. A good example of this is in action is mobile phones. 10 years ago who had a mobile phone? But today a mobile has become part of us. Corporations have spent heavily in making us perceive a mobile as an essential when in fact people survived perfectly before without one. But why am I talking about perception?

A couple of months ago I embarked on a journey to find out what exactly it means to be Black. I remembered my school days when certain students would be called 'bounty's' because of some of their characteristics so I was very interested to see what exactly people perceived made them BLACK. I found that the positive black people that I analysed had heart, passion, rhythm, soul, were hard working and were honest. Men and women like Martin Luther King, Rosa Parks, Nelson Mandela, Malcolm X, had characteristics that I believed had attributes that could be found within our people.

I looked further and found that even in things like football the players that stood out, like Thierry Henry, Ronaldo, Ronoldinho, and Okocha played with such passion and finesse that they couldn't help but stand out. But then I thought what about statistics that say young black men are the biggest academic under achievers in the UK. What about the negatives, that so plague the perception society has of my brothers. What about the idea that black girls are rude? What about things like 'Trident' that deals with black on black crime? These things are so obvious for everyone to see, and this is the other side of the spectrum. The adverse perception that is alive and kicking.

So I looked deeper and caught a revelation. One that may be controversial, but none the less I believe: – There is a view that society perceives of black people that to some extent is true. We do not help ourselves when we release and/ or support things like grime (gun crime) music and videos that glorify an image that does not aid the struggle that great men and women in the past fought for.

Martin Luther King said that he had a dream that one day we would live in a world where we were not judged by the colour of our skin but by the content of our character. I believe today his dream is alive, and the measure of each person's success lies with the determination to live positively and maintain their individuality. I also believe that there is a vicious cycle that exists within our nation and parts of this world. A cycle where by society bears a strong perception of people, and then people live up to what was labelled onto them. Sociologists call this the Labelling theory and self-fulfilling prophecy. For example if everyone thinks that all Chinese boys are good at some sort of martial art, and a Chinese boy takes up karate as a result of him subconsciously emulating a perception.

(Watch the Film Crash)
A lot of people, including a lot of Afro Caribbean's, have decided to believe in the negatives. The idea that young brothers are negative and/ or unproductive people. Teachers give up on students almost instantaneously. Old women hold tight to their bags when we walk past (even some old black senior citizens) We then conform to a way of life that is not what our skin colour says we need to be. Because you are black, it does not mean you have to screw your face. We do not have to speak substandard English.

If we grow up hearing listening and believing a perception that has been painted; the struggle will continue.

How would I tackle this issue? Stay tuned for Part 2

The Power of Perception Part 2
(May 2006)

In the first article I spoke about the perceptions that society bears of the black population, as well as how we view ourselves. I went on to identify this vicious cycle that a lot of us are trapped in that dictates our behaviour and consequently how people react to us.

Following the release of the article I received differing feedback, some from people who recognised the points that were trying to be made and others who can only be described as intimidated by the idea of truth. The truth hurts those who are so comfortable with the status quo (the way things are), some people have a "loser" mentality whereby they accept a situation, but Ghandi said that "*you* must be the change you wish to see in the world" so those of us bold enough to stand against the norms of our society should do so. Can I also confirm that I am not pro black at all, I simply recognise that how somebody perceives you they will affect how productive you can be in any given circumstance?

The answer to the question of how to tackle this problem in no uncertain terms lays in the concept 'Celebrating and elevating a positive image of ethnicity'. I used this as a mission statement in an election in Brunel University however it is more than just a mission statement. It is a way of life that I strongly believe in, a two part philosophy that I believe we should all consciously prescribe to when living our everyday lives.

The first part of the concept is celebrating. If we realise how great and rich our cultures, past and present are, we will start walking like people of worth. If you look at the Hindus for example, they celebrate their culture at least once every year (Diwali) everybody knows about the riches of their culture. They proudly dress in traditional clothing. The Hindu generations of late are highly respectable. Society sees them as 'smart' people, and in turn they fulfil that promise through attaining high employment levels in some of the greatest professions. Statistically, they are also high in the league tables of academic attainment. In regards to celebrating our current culture I believe we need to show that there are positive black people within our society. I can't help but feel that a lot of black people that go on to be a success in the corporate world seem to forget those of us that remain. Creating avenues for bankers, lawyers, doctors to plug back into the urban world would help to enforce a positive image, as well as aid in the next part of the philosophy; Elevating.

Another word that could be used for elevating is educating. 'Without education you are not going to get anywhere in life' – *(Malcolm X)*. People's mind sets and norms cannot change unless re-education takes place. Evidence that the idea of elevation works can be seen in the elections in the USA. Sean Puffy Combs 'vote or die' movement significantly improved the level of African-Americans participating in voting. As a collective, I believe there needs to be avenues whereby people that want to be positive members of society are aided in their struggle. It is very difficult to stand on your own, but if someone is at the very least encouraging you, it does help. Seminars and events need to be both regular with wider participation. Instead of waiting for the government to fix our problems why not take up the idea of autarky (self-sufficiency) and help clean up our own streets. As I said in the first article there is a vicious cycle whereby both black people and people from other backgrounds have an image based on the perceptions that so many of us so freely celebrate. We accept an idea that our culture is that of rebelliousness without really thinking. I keep hearing people saying that we need to support upcoming black artists, but if they are one of the key contributories to this problem, can someone please give me a good reason to? There are a lot of positive artists and we should support them, but it seems to me that the most notable lyrics are the ones that are part of the problem. If I was to say "I'll crack your skull, leave you f**** in a wheel chair for tryna clash ..." I'm sure you'll all know where that's from.

So where start. A lot of people have discussed and identified their own theories but have never executed their ideas sufficiently. Today (May 24th 2006), I have been elected President of the Afro Caribbean society at Brunel University, probably the largest of its kind in the U.K. I take over a society that, although it consists of the people expected to display the positive dimension of the Afro-Caribbean population, are no different from those that walk the streets. The society has an adverse image both internally and externally, which in turn repels strong minded individuals. I inherit an organisation full of division and famous for simply organising raves, a perception that regardless of level of truth still stands.

From today I embark on the journey to test the hypothesis. I anticipate struggles but as a man of the Christian faith, I'll keep hope alive to the end. So the power of perception does not just end today. Regular articles will be released from September onwards, which should be accessible through the Brunel ACS website. I encourage you all to stay tuned, and remember that though a righteous man falls seven times, he gets back up and keeps going.

The Power of Perception Part 3
(October 2006)

Following the power of perception debate on October 18th, I was approached by a young lady who had sat through the event listening. I asked her for her honest opinions as I always do, and we discussed certain issues that were raised, and things that could have been done. She then turned and asked me in the sincerest of ways, "but do you really think a change can be achieved". What a question... It made me think. What do I 'REALLY' believe? I'll give my answer later on in this article.

So this philosophy; Celebrating & Elevating a Positive Image of Ethnicity, has it worked so far? To answer this we'll go back to the first official day of the hypothesis. So it's May 25th, my first full day in charge, and my first meeting with the newly elected committee. Eleven faces, all that I know but only 1 that I speak to regularly. I sit down, nervous, not wanting to offend anyone so soon. Everyone seems to have a lot to say-besides me! They want to do this, and they want to do that, but how can I show/express to these students to scrap all their preconceived ideas because today it's operation makes a difference? 'I'M TOO INTIMIDATED BY ALL THESE FACES.'

So what do I do? I become the dream. I become the mission statement, and lead by example. I respect everyone, master the art of communication, and try my best to reflect what the society should be about. Being humble is the key to natural elevation, a true leader serves. Eventually the vision becomes a part of all.

We then move on to the new academic year. New students come on campus, and the natural segregation occurs. After a week of uncertainty, sure enough as the performance of recent years predict, the majority of the academic population find the people with the same cultural backgrounds and associate with each other. All the planning of the summer now starts to produce fruit as we have our first event. Running around trying to ensure this event runs smoothly, as it has the power to determine the success of the rest of the year, I have limited time to actually think about what I'm going to say. Close to 500 people attend the event entitled 'homecoming'. They are exposed to a new idea; a productive movement that aims to enrich anyone that comes across it. The event runs smoothly but for one incident. A young male, who I discovered does not even attend the university, decides it wise to make trouble with the security. I go to calm things down, and everything about him makes me just want to knock him out! I bite my tongue and stay calm, and the moment passes. A calm word turns away great wrath! In essence, the boy was an example of the living stereotype: the adverse perception. It made me think of my past, and times when I used to say 'talking is long, just deal with my fist!' Little did I know how ignorant I was.

It now becomes time to elevate. Operation Trident- the metropolitan black on black gun crime initiative is brought in to do a presentation about what they do. A lot of minds begin to wake up to the harsh realities of gun crime in our society. The next week we then have a Culture & Fashion show, allowing once again people to see this 'positive side of the spectrum' (Read Part one). Upon all these events I get a feeling that a lot of people were just happy that something that they've been searching for, for so long had finally been given to them. An opportunity to be black and positive without feeling like you're missing out, or sticking out like a sore thumb. A new reality was emerging.

The reason I'm re writing Part three of the saga was the Power of Perception debate. I thank God for the lives of everybody that attended and contributed that day. I learnt so much from so many people. Finally a platform to see what really lays beneath so many people's personas. Issues were addressed, as a people, however minute we were in compar- ison to the greater population, we were still able to stand together to address issues that shouldn't exist, but do, like the colour of your skin having the potential power to place you in a category.

The wisdom flowing out of some of these young people's

mouths was so special. History going back to slavery days, like William Lynch's mental slavery philosophy of divide and rule. I was inspired/ convicted to know more, and most importantly to read more. Knowledge is power (if applied), so many people either lack knowledge because they do not search for it, or they simply do not apply the knowledge they have.

The art of a nonconformist is in the name, but one can only think, will these same people who were so passionate at the debate, be strong enough to stand outside. At the moment, the sad truth is that, for the majority, the answer is probably no. Not because they're bad people, but they fail to understand the concept of helping each other. Someone said in the debate 'together we stand, divided we fall'. That statement bares so much truth. In the Civil Rights Movement in America, students with an issue founded an organisation- (Student Non-violent Coordination Committee-SNCC) – at such a tough time, where standing alone would have been near impossible. They were able to stand together, and do their part for their struggle. STUDENTS! We live in a selfish generation, everyone has their own agendas, 'I want to own this', and 'I want to go there'. The fact that I'm even focusing on this issue in one of the richest countries in the world could be argued to be selfish altogether. People are dying in other corners of the world and us- the lucky ones- cannot even master the art of being positive!

So do I in my heart of hearts think that a significant impact could be made? To find this answer I had to search my heart very deeply. The word that evaluates every single piece of success achieved on earth is the answer to her question- FAITH- The hope of things to come- the evidence of things not seen. The same way I believe a change can be made, is the same way Orville and Wilbur Wright had the belief that they could create the aeroplane. If man can fly, then can they not learn how to overcome a problem as simple as perception?

189

So, a critique on the thesis so far: in terms of the study itself a criticism for me would be that enough hasn't been done to 'Celebrate' this positive image.

Until part four stay positive as I leave you with the words a young lady said to me when I was very close to giving up; THERE'S HOPE AMONGST THE MADNESS OF THE MASSES!

Afterword

I have held an interest in history and politics from childhood and my involvement in conservative politics began, I am sure, as a natural following. My Grandmother, a highly spirited cockney, had been a volunteer assistant to Margaret Thatcher's 1959 campaign in Finchley when she first stood as an MP, and for every election thereafter. In hindsight it is probably her inspiration that drew me from interest to practice.

It is easy to fall into the trap of just being a "Conservative" and become railroaded towards a certain finite world view. What is best for the country is best wherever and whoever it comes from. I am and will always be a patriot first and foremost, and often party politics can blind one to the original beliefs that took one into politics in the first place. It is perhaps the sole advantage of the young politician, often wanting in experience, to still retain some of that original drive.

I can accept the dissolution of the Conservative Party, if that so happens, a party will at least drift in and out of power as is natural in any democracy, but I cannot accept the decline of Great Britain. It is a country which I will always be patriotically proud to call home, but to be coldly objective I cannot accept it because I now have a real stake in it. That stake is by virtue of my belief in a conservative and a British way of life; it's a stake that every nation should grant its citizens, and every citizen should accept in full understanding of its responsibility.

As many people of my generation, I had the opportunity to go to college and university where my parents and their parents did not, but also to do so relatively cheaply by comparison to today's student body. It is an opportunity I felt obliged to take. I studied A levels at college in Cambridge, and later attended the University of Strasbourg in France and then the London School of Economics to study Politics, Economics and International Relations. Following University I worked abroad for several years before returning to London to take up the Chairmanship of the Bow Group, the UK's oldest conservative think tank.

I see conservatism as a belief that traditional values of sanctity of family, of individual property, of community and of nationhood are paramount in building a strong society. Central also is a belief that every citizen must be free to attain by will all that they wish and all that they are able to by merit, without excessive taxation or subjugation by the state.

That does not by philosophy advocate wanton and destructive greed. It is the belief in the necessity of the freedom of the individual before the state, but not before one's own inherited responsibility. To use a sporting analogy, an athlete may compete viscously, aggressively, tirelessly against foreign counterparts, but never against one's home nation.

If these are also your views, then you have as great a claim to conservatism as any.

The Bow Group has always been an organisation populated largely by young people who wish to engage with politics. As Chairman of the Bow Group it is my role to engage the younger generation with conservative politics, and to engage the Conservative Party with the issues as we see them. It is important to note however that at its core conservatism, in the UK or anywhere else, is a philosophy: It is not and does not have to be focussed or tied to the Conservative Party.

The people for whom low growth, increasing government debt, and high unemployment, should be the most sobering news are those who most often exhibit the least concern and political engagement, and have the smallest voice when policy is being made, often because they are concerned about the issues, but turned off by political parties.

Young people in Britain, more than any other demographic grouping, should be deeply concerned by the nation's economic future and position in the world, and must be strongly politically engaged on that basis. The harsh reality for those born in Britain in the 21st century is that unless they are fortunate enough to be born into wealth and privilege, freedom to work, own property and reach aspirations will depend increasingly on luck and less on hard work and ability than it did 30 years ago. As a generation, the young people of today will be working less, earning less, owning less and paying the government much, much more throughout their lives than their parents did, chiefly to service a debt legacy that they were not responsible for, nor benefitted from. The only truly visible concern and reaction to this that the nation has seen from its youth thus far are violent student and anti-cuts protests, and riots, a perspective that is sadly and worryingly wrong in both philosophy and execution.

For young people from African Caribbean backgrounds the issues around lack of political engagement are far more severe, and even within the younger demographic, Bow Group research shows that young people from African Caribbean backgrounds will be among those hit hardest by the recession of the 2000's. Yet only 16 percent of all ethnic minorities voted Conservative at the last general election; it cannot be that only 16 percent of ethnic minorities want lower taxes, lower debts, responsible budgets, family values and a smaller state. A recent survey commissioned by the Runnymede Trust demonstrated that people from African Caribbean backgrounds are the group least likely to vote Conservative, and our studies show a similar disengagement with government as a whole.

A 2012 Bow Group & Elevation Networks study entitled "Race to the Top", designed to research and analyse the views and attitudes of young Black students found that there was huge support for policies supporting lower taxes, prioritisation of family values, individual freedoms coupled with a highly aspirational and acquisitive outlook, but when those policies were identified as those of the Conservative Party the cultural barrier became apparent. The Conservative Party was seen as being that which much of the media seeks to portray, not only not inclusive or open to all backgrounds, but made up of utterly distasteful individuals entirely foreign from normality. Another perception held equally was that politicians were disingenuous, paying only lip service to widening engagement beyond a shallow elite for electoral purposes, and therefore willing to sacrifice any principle or policy for political gain.

What our study also found is that young black students believe, there is bias against their applications to become involved in politics or the political process. From my experience, and from that of the Bow Group, I do not believe there is, but the problem remains significant, as for many students perception is reality, and deters application and engagement with the wider political process.

As we moved into the new millennium I believed we were largely living in a Britain of a post-racial society, and that opportunity was no longer decided by virtue of race. In my experience this has also been the common belief of many of my peers. I firmly believe that excellence, not equality, should be the quarry of our universities, our economy, our Parliament and our society, and that there is no place in conservative thought for state imposed quotas or positive discrimination. What I learned in the process of the Bow Group's study, however, was that the issue has greater nuance, and that much more work is required to ensure people from all backgrounds are able to get involved in conservative politics, and perhaps more importantly, want to.

The long term result of a perception of young people and those from ethnic minority backgrounds that, while their views and beliefs may be conservative, the Conservative Party is foreign and opposed to them as individuals, is of grave severity. It will surely dissuade the most qualified people from getting involved in politics at a young age, perhaps forever. This is particularly evident for young women who seem even less inclined to play the high skulduggery, low stakes game of student and youth politics, which has often served as a natural feeder for the national political debate. It also means that the debate in universities, work-places, and the nation as a whole will be increasingly dominated by militant socialists operating with a union handbook who have, to their small credit, been far more able to vocalise support among British youth for policies which will drive the United Kingdom into further debt and economic turmoil.

The first problem with lack of engagement I deem to be a social one; the Conservative Party, and politics in general, is still seen as an arena that is not for young people and not for ethnic minorities. It is therefore going to take a huge amount of courage for an individual to knock on the great doors of Westminster, with the perception that they will be the first and only one of their background inside. The social structure of the Conservative Party has changed significantly in my life-time, and often to become more welcoming to those from a wider variety of backgrounds. If anything the focus on that change has become too significant and led to an almost Stasiesque approach to managing local Conservative Associations and Party members output by Conservative Party Headquarters, and attempting to push public opinion with hollow initiatives like the failed "A-list".

I feel the best way to tackle any negative perception of the Conservative Party socially, and to increase the Party's national appeal and engagement, is to take the same approach as the Party took in the 1980's. To lead with conservative policy and a vision for Britain, and to be unfailingly clear and distinct as to the direction of that policy. The Conservative Party has garnered support among vast swathes of non traditional Tory voters in the past not by modifying or diluting policies to appeal to polled groups, but by standing resolutely by them and making the movement about nothing else but them.

There is a great danger, for the party, and the country, that the Conservative Party makes the mistake of assuming a change to its social structure necessitates or equates to movement in its policy away from values traditionally considered as conservative. The movement to modernise the Party under David Cameron since 2005 has consistently made the fundamental error of assuming conservative ideology or policies are the problem; they are not, they are the solution.

The second problem is that the post racial view of full equality of opportunity is desirable, but we must accept it has not been achieved. I don't believe this process is best served by the top down approaches we have seen from political parties in the past, of press-ganging and exploiting minority candidates before an election simply to meet quotas and fulfil what is deemed to be a necessary public image. Work must begin much earlier, at school level, to ensure that those from non traditional backgrounds are given the right guidance to move into a political life.

The Bow Group & Elevation Networks recommended in the "Race to the Top" study that provisions are made to ensure that the nation's best Universities, companies and political parties offer mentoring at pre GCSE level in **all** schools, to better guide students towards excellence in their chosen paths.

These programmes are within the power and gift of the British Government and British institutions like the Conservative Party, but these are also their limitations.

It is up to every individual that is born in Great Britain to ask themselves what they want, and equally what they can offer, and we together must ask ourselves what we want to be as a nation and where we want to go in the future. If you feel that you hold political views and wish to have a voice, it is a journey in which barriers can no longer be accepted or respected.

In this cause you are important and you are needed, but no other person can be relied upon to stand up for you and make your case, nothing of value will ever be handed to you for free or without struggle, your greatest fortune you have already, as a citizen of Great Britain.

Ben Harris-Quinney
Chairman, The Bow Group

About The Bow Group:
Founded in 1951, The Bow Group is the oldest conservative think tank in Britain. It holds no corporate view, and is thus open to all strands of conservative thought. Although often associated with the Conservative party, the group is an independent organisation. The Bow Group exists to publish and promote the research and policy proposals of its members, through policy papers, policy briefs and larger collaborative projects. Its members are predominantly people in their 20s and 30s, and also include leading Conservative politicians. A major influence on Conservative Party policy for many years, the group is again attracting notice as a source of fresh ideas on public services, welfare, the condition of our inner cities and crime policy.